OXFORDSHIRE CO

5

GLYME VALLEY

WOODSTOCK TO CHIPPING NORTON

MARY WEBB   ALAN SPICER
ALLISTER SMITH

Illustrated by LOUISE SPICER

THE
aRTISAN
PRESS

The Artisan Press (Publishers) Limited

This book is dedicated to Roland Pomfret who lived
at Wootton in the Glyme Valley and did so much to preserve
the Rights of Way network throughout Oxfordshire

Cover photograph: The Glyme Valley viewed from Stratford Bridge,
Wootton (Alan Spicer)

PUBLISHER'S NOTE

The routes of the walks in this book all follow definitive rights of way
and have been checked by Oxfordshire County Council's Countryside
Service. It is advisable for walkers to use the latest edition of the
relevant Ordnance Survey Pathfinder Series 1:25000 scale maps to
follow the route of the walks. Diversions to the definitive right of way
may occur and walkers should look out for signs notifying official
diversions. Enquiries regarding rights of way should be addressed to
the Countryside Service, Oxfordshire County Council, Holton, Oxford
OX33 1QQ

Oxfordshire Country Walks – Vol. 5: Glyme Valley
ISBN 0 9529238 1 5
First published in 1997 by The Artisan Press (Publishers) Ltd
Copyright © 1997 The Artisan Press (Publishers) Ltd

A CIP catalogue record for this book is available from the British Library.

Typesetting and origination by The Artisan Press (Publishers) Ltd.
Printed by Information Press Ltd., Oxford

The Artisan Press (Publishers) Ltd
PO Box 1098, Winscombe, Bristol BS25 1DT
and The Studio, Sheep Street, Charlbury, Oxon OX7 3RR

Contents

Preface   4

Introduction   5

Location of the walks   22

THE WALKS

1 **Wootton** 5.5 miles (9km)   25

2 **Glympton and Kiddington** 6.5 miles (10.5km)   41

3 **Enstone and Ditchley** 7.5 miles (12km)   55

4 **Heythrop** 4.5 miles (7km)   71

5 **Lidstone** 5.5 miles (9km)   83

6 **Chadlington** 8 miles (13km)   97

7 **Chipping Norton** 7.5 miles (12km)   109

8 **Salford and Little Rollright** 7 miles (11km)   123

Acknowledgements   136

Foreword

The Oxfordshire Branch of the Council for the Protection of Rural England is part of a national charity dedicated to the protection of the countryside. Our work includes the monitoring of the rights of way throughout the county and we collaborate with Oxfordshire County Council to ensure that walkers and riders can continue to enjoy unimpeded access to our beautiful countryside. We are proud to have played a leading part in securing the first two long distance footpaths in Oxfordshire – the d'Arcy Dalton Way and the Oxfordshire Way; our support towards the publication of this book is a new venture for us in the promotion to the general public of the delights of exploring the county by walking on the footpath network.

Much of the CPRE's work is concerned with the planning system, trying to ensure modern development does not destroy those aspects of the countryside which are important to us all. We are anxious to promote methods of farming and other rural industries which respect and enhance the environment. Currently we are recording the pattern of hedgerows in the county to aid their protection; we are members of the Oxfordshire Nature Conservation Forum and are lending our support to the project to recreate Wychwood Forest, parts of which are covered by this book.

HUGO BRUNNER
Lord Lieutenant and Patron of CPRE Oxfordshire Branch

If you would like to join CPRE you will find an application form inside this book. For further information please contact:

**CPRE Oxfordshire Branch, Freepost, Priestley's Loft,
The Barn House, Church Hanborough, Witney, Oxon OX8 8AB.
Telephone: 01993 883659**

CPRE

Your countryside – your voice

Preface

This series of circular walks explores a quiet, undiscovered part of west Oxfordshire covering the area between Woodstock and Chipping Norton, focusing on the River Glyme valley, and extending to Chadlington in the west and Rollright on the county border to the north-west.

The length of the walks varies from 3 to 8 miles (5 to 13 km) and short cuts are included where possible. The terrain is generally undulating with some steeper climbs so the going is quite easy. Some paths tend to be muddy in wet weather. The time taken to follow the routes will vary with the individual, but the routes are designed to be taken at a leisurely pace to allow plenty of time to read the descriptions and to enjoy the wildlife and landscape along the way. Ordnance survey maps (1:25000) will add to the interest of the walks and grid references have been given for each numbered section of the route desriptions.

The guide has been produced with the aim of showing how much of our history, both human and natural, is present in the landscape. Features such as prehistoric standing stones, Roman roads, deserted medieval settlements and 18th century landscaped grounds are still to be seen within the context of a modern agricultural landscape, which also contains areas of more natural habitats. The introduction gives a brief overview of the history of the landscape and its wildlife value.

Walking in the countryside is an enjoyable leisure activity but readers should be aware that all outdoor pursuits carry certain risks. The authors cannot accept responsibility for damage or injury to individuals or property occasioned by following the routes recommended in this book.

We hope you enjoy discovering this little-known landscape, as much as we enjoyed producing this book.

Introduction

This book covers an area between Woodstock and Chipping Norton, loosely focusing on the River Glyme valley and on the hills around Chipping Norton. Although close in distance, these two areas have distinct landscapes, resulting from differences in landform and historical use.

GEOLOGY

The geology of a district directly affects the appearance of the landscape, by influencing the landform (topography), settlement patterns, agriculture, communication routes and building materials.

The underlying rock of the area covered by this book is Great Oolite Limestone Formation. The rock was formed about 165 million years ago during the Jurassic Period when most of southern Britain was covered by shallow, warm sea. At this time a variety of carbonate sediments, including oolites, minute spherical particles of calcium carbonate, were laid down on previously deposited layers of deeper water dark muds, which are now known as the Lias Clays. Today these clays are found in the river valleys, where the action of flowing water has cut through the layer of limestone and exposed the underlying softer strata. It is certain that the rivers of the area were much larger in the recent past than now when they carried the melt water after the end of the last Ice Age about 12,000 years ago, thus cutting the river valleys we see now, characterising this landscape of hills and valleys.

The free-draining limestone allows water to percolate

through while the impermeable clay prevents it from penetrating further, thus causing springs to emerge at the junction between the two layers. Sometimes these can be seen in various places along the routes; if you are using an Ordnance Survey 1:25000 map you will see springs marked along the valleys. Early settlements often grew up close to springs, because their water supply was more constant compared to the fluctuating levels of streams and rivers. Chipping Norton is a good example of a large springline settlement but there are others such as Lidstone and Little Rollright.

The dry limestone uplands were traditionally favoured for sheep grazing and arable crops while the damper clay valleys, often prone to flooding, were more productive as meadow land for hay or for the grazing of dairy cattle which can tolerate wetter conditions underfoot.

The Great Oolite Limestones were, and are, commonly used in construction, both locally and for many major Oxfordshire buildings including Blenheim Palace, Magdalen Bridge and Tower, the Ruskin School of Drawing and part of the Radcliffe Camera in Oxford, as well as for the field walls in much of this region. The Cotswold area is typified by the light, golden colour of the stone; this is the "signature" for the region and illustrates how the underlying rock strata dictate the appearance of both the natural and built landscape.

LANDSCAPE HISTORY

Like almost every part of England, there is a continuity of at least 5,000 years in human occupation of the Glyme valley area. Most inhabitants, but not all, have left a mark on the landscape and some have made a greater impact than others.

Lost Landscape

There are few monuments to pre-historic man in this area, but those that remain are impressive, bearing in mind their primitive equipment. The Hoar Stone at Enstone and the Whispering Knights at Rollright are remains of Neolithic or possibly even earlier Megalithic burial chambers, but the other standing stones at

Rollright indicate a later complex society needing
a meeting place and religious ceremonies (Walks 3
and 8). The Iron Age leaves its mark as earthworks,
Knollbury near Chadlington and Grim's Ditch, a linear
bank and ditch which crosses several parishes in the area
and was possibly built as a defence against the Romans
or as a territorial boundary. (Walks 6 and 2).

The Whispering Knights

For several centuries the Romans had a strong
presence in the wider area, the well-drained soil allowing
intensive agriculture. Akeman Street was an important
road linking east and west and passes near Wootton
where Walk 1 crosses it twice. There were many villas
in the area (Walk 2) which ranged from simple farms to
grand houses, and although none survive, it is estimated
that much of this landscape was under cultivation.

After the Roman decline by the end of the 4th century
AD, much of their cultivated land reverted back to rough
land with scrub and trees. Part of this area eventually
became the Royal Forest of Wychwood and was
recorded as such in the Domesday Book in 1086. The
term "Royal Forest" refers to land, not necessarily tree-
covered, which belonged to the King, where he or
another important person had the right to keep deer and
to make Forest Laws (see Book 1). Some of the walks
in this book include the borders of the old Royal Forest
particularly Walks 1 and 3. An Anglo-Saxon royal
estate was centred on Wootton and later Woodstock
where, by 1000 AD, there was a hunting park in the area
which much later became Blenheim Park.

Many of the villages seen today had their roots in the Anglo-Saxon period. Agriculture developed as a system of two or three large open-fields which were cultivated in rotation, leaving one fallow or uncultivated every year to maintain fertility, to reduce weeds and for grazing. For example, in 1266 Chadlington had two fields, each of 27 acres. Fields were farmed in common, meaning that all the villagers shared the land, which was allotted in strips to each family. Repeated ploughing over time by cumbersome ox ploughs built up a system of ridges and furrows in the soil which aided drainage. On steeper ground ploughing across the slope resulted in terraces or lynchets (Walk 7).

In some places cultivation was already on a large scale by the time the parish boundaries were demarcated, several centuries before the Norman conquest in 1066. This resulted in a zig-zag parish boundary, usually only visible now as a line of dots on a map. In other places woodland was still being cleared well into the 13th century as the need for agricultural land increased. Often this new land was not incorporated into the open fields but left as smaller, hedged fields. By the end of the 13th century expansion had reached its highest point with a high population but during the next century the landscape changed dramatically in many parts of this area.

The Working Landscape

The early 14th century brought change to many parts of the country and this part of Oxfordshire was no exception. There was a series of bad harvests and poor weather which led to hardship and disease amongst animals as well as people. There was a gradual change in the system of farming with the lords taking a more direct interest in the running of their estates. The Black Death or bubonic plague epidemic which started in 1348 reduced the population considerably. This resulted in some villages and hamlets gradually being deserted altogether like Broadstone and Nether Chalford (Walk 5), Boriens (Walk 2), and Asterleigh (Walk 3). In other places the large arable open fields were inclosed and made into sheep pasture. Sheep husbandry needed less labour and the wool brought high returns for the landowner. These are the fields which have not been ploughed since and which still show the pattern of ridge-and-furrow, preserved in the grass. Of course, many fields have lost this formation through later ploughing, but can still be identified by their large square shape and old hedges (Walk 8).

These changes continued slowly over the next two or three centuries but not everywhere in the region. Many parishes remained as open fields until the 18th and 19th centuries, but by then inclosure started to take place in these parishes too. Improvements in agriculture and the start of mechanisation meant that crop yields could be improved by a more efficient way of farming, so landowners pressed for change. By this time inclosure had to be approved by an Act of Parliament, first on an individual basis, parish by parish, but by 1845 there was a General Inclosure Act which speeded up the process. This wave of inclosures led to the landscape changing again. The fields were laid out in an even, rectangular pattern with newly planted hawthorn hedges or stone walls. New, isolated farms were built amongst the fields, away from the villages (Walk 6). The road system was often changed too; earlier inclosure left roads with wide verges to compensate for loss of grazing and poor surfaces, but later ones had narrower verges as the road surfaces improved.

One benefit for local people which resulted from late inclosures was the provision of allotments. These were given to compensate for the loss of land on which poor people could grow vegetables or keep a cow or pig. In the late 19th and early 20th century they were a very important part of village life but now in many places are greatly under-used.

The changes brought by inclosure in the 14th and 15th and the 18th and 19th centuries formed much of the landscape we see today along these paths. However there was another source of change which was not so much for profit as for pleasure.

Landscape of Pleasure

Since Roman times this part of North Oxfordshire has been favoured as a desirable district for the well-to-do. Within the area covered by these walks there are six post-Tudor mansions and landscaped parks, the most magnificent, of course, being Blenheim Palace. Most replace older houses and walled parks which were on the same sites. All except Sarsden House are close to the River Glyme or its valley; three houses, Kiddington, Glympton and Blenheim, all have lakes and cascades formed by damming the river. There was no room for the ordinary populace in these schemes; three villages, Heythrop, Glympton and Old Woodstock were moved to make way for parks.

During the 17th and 18th centuries, the wealthy became interested in new ideas in agricultural improvement, which led, not only to the Parliamentary Inclosures described above, but also to a desire for an idealised "improved" natural landscape in which to set

Blenheim Park

their new grand houses. Prior to this period, "nature" was kept well away from houses which were surrounded by walled formal gardens in which trees were shaped by clipping and flowers were planted in formal arrangements. The new ideas were inspired by landscape designers such as Capability Brown, whose first of many Oxfordshire contracts was at Kiddington Hall in 1740 when he was 24 years old.

The landscapes at Glympton, Kiddington, Ditchley and Blenheim were designed by Capability Brown, at Heythrop by Thomas Archer and at Sarsden by Humphrey Repton. These designers spanned more than 100 years, ideas and fashions evolving over this period. They all created an idealised natural or picturesque landscape with smooth rolling grassland, groups of trees, areas of "wilderness" with winding paths through dense shrubbery, and ornamental lakes, often winding between contoured slopes and formed by a dammed river or stream. Often large specimen trees, some new exotic species from America and the Far East, were planted in order to create the desired effect.

Now all the landscapes have matured and changed since they were first made but their concept is still obvious. This is a very English style of garden design, not found in other parts of Europe, and is a marked contrast to the ordered agricultural landscape outside the boundaries of the parks.

If you follow these trails in numerical order you will see that the first four walks travel through this landscape of parks. Walks 7 and 8 explore mainly the landscape of early and Parliamentary inclosure while Walks 5 and 6 allow you to contrast both types of landscape in one route.

Landscape of the Present

The landscape along all the routes is influenced by modern pressures, which sometimes seems to obliterate all signs of the past. However if you look carefully, you will see that today's landscape is a mosaic of fragments from all the previous periods, but overlain by modern influences.

Post-war intensive farming led to the removal of many hedges to make way for more crops and large machinery, which in effect gives a taste of the medieval open-field landscape. This is now beginning to change again with new hedges and small copses being planted to provide shelter for crops and game and to reduce the amount of arable land under production. Modern arable methods have been so successful that there is a glut of produce so that farmers are encouraged to take land out of production into set-aside. This leads to changes in the traditional landscape with bare set-aside fields in summer instead of winter when cultivated fields are green with the autumn-sown crops giving a lawn-like appearance. In some places you may see new uses for agricultural land such as golf courses and horse paddocks. Even the animals in the fields are different, with a far wider range of cattle than the former black and white Friesians which were such a common sight. This diversification is a way of making a living from the land without producing more unwanted crops.

Villages have changed as well. Now most people living in the countryside work in towns, often commuting for long distances. The old cottages have mostly been modernised and other old buildings like barns, mills and chapels are now living accommodation. Modern houses are often constructed with non-local materials so that the traditional local character is being diminished, although now planning regulations are stricter than in the 1960's and 70's, so hopefully preventing too much inappropriate development. Farms often contain a mixture of traditional and modern buildings, ranging from Cotswold stone barns to metal fabricated cattle sheds and vehicle stores.

Local industries

On a local scale, the landscape has a part to play in industries which historically made use of materials which were close at hand.

As mentioned above, the Oolitic limestone was used extensively for building so that there was quite a large quarrying industry throughout the region. The main

13

quarries such as that at Taynton near Burford were outside the immediate area covered by this book, but there are numerous overgrown small quarries which provided stone for village use (Walks 5 and 6).

An obvious spin-off from the large medieval sheep pastures is the woollen trade which was a staple for Chipping Norton for several centuries. By the 15th century wool had brought wealth to the town; this is reflected in the interior of the church which was rebuilt by a wool merchant around that time. Various types of cloth were manufactured and by the early 19th century tweed production began at the mill owned by Bliss and Son, which was established during the 18th century. The mill was rebuilt after a fire in 1872 in a grand style which was intended to resemble a mansion in landscaped grounds. It remained in operation until 1980. Now the facade remains but the building has been transformed into apartments.

Another industry reliant on local livestock was that of glove-making. Leather was made in the region from sheepskin and deerskin, the latter coming from animals in the Royal Forest of Wychwood. There was a Glovers Gild in Oxford in 1461 but later this craft was mainly concentrated in the villages and towns around Wychwood Forest which included Chipping Norton, Woodstock and Wootton. The leather was cut by the men, but the women sewed the gloves which were finished off by children tying the threads at the end of the fingers. As with most cottage craft industries the coming of automation at the end of the 19th century ended employment for small producers.

Communications

Many of the footpaths used now for recreation were more important in the past as a means of linking villages with each other or with the fields or pastures. Some tracks, shown on old maps such as that made by Richard Davis in 1797, are now tarred roads, but many are still just footpaths or have been altered by the new layout brought by inclosures (see Walk 6).

Some tracks or green lanes were very important in

the past. The Salt Way (Walk 8) was part of a long distance network, which transported the salt produced from the brine springs in the Droitwich area to Oxfordshire and Buckinghamshire. Salt was a sought-after commodity during the Middle Ages as it was the only means of food preservation. The track would have been used by other traffic but salt must have been a notable part of this usage. Other roads from Chipping Norton are also identified as Saltways, for example the A361 (Walk 6).

This and other tracks such as Dornford Lane (Walk 1) were later used as drove roads for animals going to the large markets around London. Animals travelled from Wales and the North of England and were sold to be fattened after their long journeys. From the 17th century drovers used these tracks as a means of avoiding tolls which were charged on the main roads which had been improved by the Turnpike Trusts. Prior to the setting up of Turnpikes, roads were in a very poor state and Trusts were set up to improve them. It was an early form of privatisation with investments being made by local dignitaries and profits and maintenance being funded by the tolls. Animals were charged per head so tolls could take much of their earnings away from the drovers. The Turnpikes mainly utilised roads already in existence and many are now modern main roads. However some routes have declined, for example, the quiet road through Glympton was once part of the turnpike between London and Aberystwyth.

Railways have no modern impact on this landscape, but the line through Chipping Norton was important in the later 19th century, particularly as a means of transporting cloth and gloves from the area. The disused line is now disappearing under shrubs and trees, good for wildlife but not for human communication!

Hedges in the landscape

Hedges are not only an important wildlife habitat but are also a good indicator of past landscape history. The Parliamentary inclosures of the 18th and 19th centuries culminated in a massive hedge planting operation, although in this area, some stone walls were built instead. Hawthorn was mostly used for these new hedges; a strong, animal-proof shrub, which has been used for hedging for many centuries. Its name comes from the Old English word *haga* – hedge. These late inclosure hedges are easy to identify as they are predominately still composed of hawthorn.

The hedges planted around the earlier 14th and 15th century sheep pastures look very different. These hedges are now about five or six hundred years old; this length of time has allowed a mixture of species to colonise the hedges which were probably planted with whatever species came to hand, although hawthorn may have been dominant then as well. A rule of thumb is that the number of species in a thirty yard/metre length of hedge represents approximately 100 years in age. Therefore if six shrub species are found then the hedge will be about 600 years old. This estimate must be treated with care as increasingly replacement modern hedges are being planted with mixed species beneficial to wildlife.

A third type of hedge is that found in places where fields were taken out of woodland but not incorporated into the open field. These hedges would have been made up of woodland shrubs, left in place to form a barrier. They will contain mixed shrub species but in addition will have woodland plants growing beneath them, such as dog's mercury, bluebell or yellow archangel. Hedges formed in this way will confuse the dating formula mentioned above so it is important to get other historical data to confirm the age of a hedge.

THE WILDLIFE OF THE GLYME VALLEY

The Glyme valley has a predominantly agricultural landscape, but within this countryside are fragments of natural or semi-natural grassland, woodland and wetland habitats. These remnants have survived either because they are situated in places where cultivation would be difficult, for example in wet valley floors or on steep hills, or because through an accident of history, a small area has been untouched by modern methods. The different light, temperature and moisture conditions within these habitats affects the diversity of plant and animal species to be found there, so enhancing the wildlife value of the area.

Grassland

Grassland is a conspicuous feature of the area but grasslands are not all the same. Most are improved agricultural grass, used for silage, hay or grazing, but in a few places unimproved flower-rich grassland can be found which has survived, untouched by pesticides, artificial fertiliser, ploughing or drainage. Different plants and animals will be found in all types of grassland, but those places with the least disturbed conditions will support the greatest diversity of wildlife.

Some unimproved grassland is found in damp meadows alongside the river. Here plants will be those which like often water logged conditions, whereas those growing on the steep drier limestone slopes can tolerate a frequent lack of water and an alkaline soil. Other places where unimproved limestone grassland can be found are along many of the verges bordering tracks, lanes and roads.

These have often escaped the effects of treatments applied to neighbouring fields and are a haven for flowers, which in turn attract an abundance of insects such as butterflies, moths and bees. Another source of unspoilt grassland can often be found in country churchyards which contain small areas of flowery turf.

These habitats all display the type of flora which would have been commonplace half a century ago and now it is important that these now often rare grasslands are conserved. BBONT, the Berkshire, Buckinghamshire and Oxfordshire Naturalists' Trust, often manages sites such as those along the River Glyme (Walk 7) ensuring that the land use does not clash with the conservation interest of the sites. Some road verges are designated as nature reserves by the County Council, which has a responsibility to care for them. The grass will be mowed but at the right time of year to encourage the flowering plants. An increasing number of community groups or parish councils are being helped through the "Rural Action for the Environment" project to conserve the wildlife interest of their churchyards or other parts of their parish by sensitive management.

Farming and Wildlife

Apart from the landscaped grounds surrounding the large houses, the countryside of the Glyme valley and the surrounding ridges is mainly farmland. During the last fifty years, most of the fields have been improved to increase yields of crops and farm animals. In relatively recent times, changes in farming practices have had dramatic effects upon the landscape. In particular the development of winter sown crop varieties has meant that winter landscapes of ploughed, brown fields are not common now as growing crops turn the fields green. At other times of year, land removed from cultivation under set-aside schemes appear as odd patches of rough vegetation in otherwise intensively managed areas. These new practices have both advantageous and disadvantageous effects upon wildlife. Some birds, such as woodpigeons, benefit considerably from having green crops to feed on for much of the year, and some finches and seed-eating birds use the seed heads from grasses and other plants in set-aside fields. On the other hand, ground nesting birds have suffered from changed planting patterns. The well-grown crops in spring make it difficult for them to find nest sites, to see approaching danger and the young birds have difficulties struggling through the lush growth.

However despite these changes, small areas of natural, unimproved flower-rich grasslands and marsh remain, which can be conserved by landowners refraining from intensification. Better still, by using more traditional ways of grazing and mowing, the diversity and abundance of the wildlife in such places may be increased. Recently the Glyme valley has been designated part of the Upper Thames Tributaries Environmentally Sensitive Area (ESA). Grants may now be available to help landowners increase the biodiversity of fields bordering the River Glyme by supporting traditional, less profitable farming methods.

Another source of help is the Farming and Wildlife Advisory Group (FWAG) for Oxfordshire. Its officers advise landowners on the maintenance and creation of habitats on farmland to maximise their wildlife interest. Care of hedgerows and the planting of hedges and small woodlands, careful management of field edges and track verges, restoration and creation of new ponds can all help to increase the diversity of wildlife in the countryside.

Woodland

There are some sizable remnants of the ancient broadleaf Royal Forest of Wychwood in this area (see Walks 2 and 6). Here oak, ash, field maple and other trees support old communities of lower plants including ferns, mosses lichens and fungi while a great variety of insects inhabit the surfaces and crevices of the tree bark. Insect-eating birds are attracted to these ancient woodlands and many of the flowering plants are only found in such old woodlands or survive in hedges left behind when woodland was cleared or assarted. Many of the woodlands and former copses of Ditchley and Kiddington estates have been felled and replanted with conifers, sometimes mixed with beech, for commercial forestry. The dense shade created by such trees prevents the woodland plants from flowering except in the rides or paths left between the blocks of woodland. However, when these commercial trees are cut down for timber, replanting with traditional broadleaf trees and, better still, maintenance of a coppicing cycle by cutting down areas within the woodland every 10 or 15 years, could restore the woodland's botanical diversity.

Many of the small woodlands in this area were planted as refuges for game such as pheasants and foxes. Other animals and birds have taken up residence and would undoubtedly be less plentiful if these copses were missing from the countryside.

Wetlands

Wetlands vary from flowing rivers and streams to still ponds and lakes to marshy waterlogged ground bordering watercourses. Water is a conspicuous feature of this area and adds an important seasonal element to the walks in this book. Walks in wet winter conditions will reveal flooded and waterlogged fields whereas in summer gentle rivers, village and farm ponds, and estate lakes will be noticeable features. Open water, the submerged environment, and the banks all provide different wetland habitats and these natural differences, so evident along streamsides and pond edges, have been adopted by formal estate gardeners in the careful choice of plant types able to withstand varying degrees of soil moisture.

Wildlife Diversity

Add to the obvious habitats outlined above others such as ornamental parkland, cottage gardens, churchyards, *River Glyme*

St. Kenelm's Church, Enstone

quarries, old orchards, and even the stonework in walls and buildings to discover that a surprisingly large variety of habitats can be found in a relatively small area of countryside.

Even greater variation can be found when the physical conditions of each site are taken into account. Factors like sun and shade, moisture levels, soil depth, relative acidity or alkalinity and many more, may result in an almost infinite range of conditions suitable to support collections of wildlife.

This tremendous variation in habitats leads to a great diversity in the range of creatures and plants that can flourish in such a river valley and its surrounding hills. As you walk through this area, look out for these differences, some obvious, some subtle, and for the corresponding changes they evoke in the wildlife to be found.

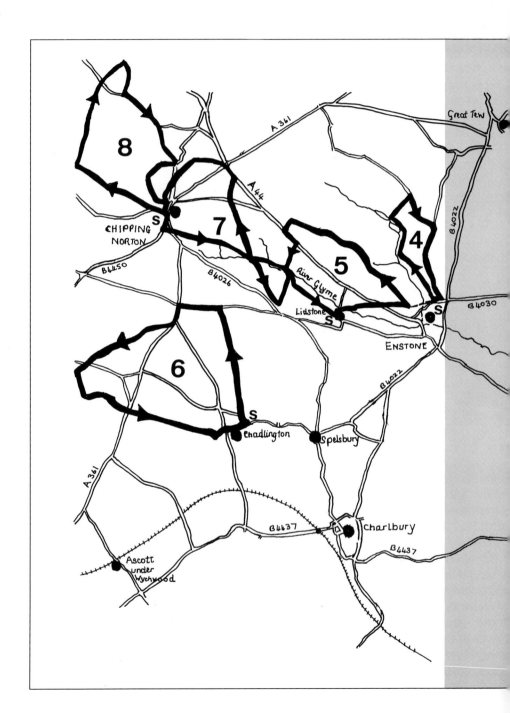

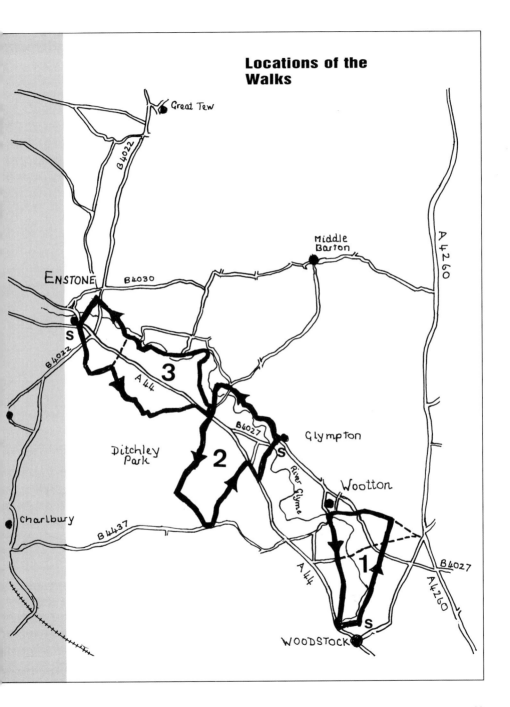

Locations of the Walks

23

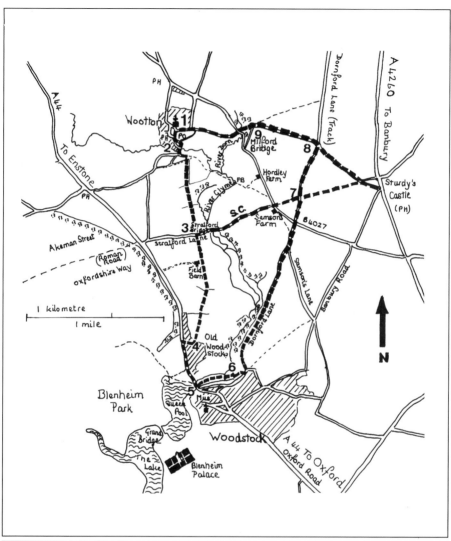

Key to individual route maps

Key (legend):

Road	Building	NT	National Trust
Circular Walk	Residential		Railway line
Walk on road	Deciduous trees	Spr	Spring
Track	Conifers	F B	Footbridge
Footpath	Grassland	SC	Short cut
Stream or River	Church	A R	Alternative route
Pond or lake	PH	Public House	

Wootton

5.5 miles 9 km

Short cut 3 miles 5 km

This walk between the attractive village of Wootton and the historic town of Woodstock, follows old tracks and green roads overlooking the peaceful Glyme valley. The paths are mostly level but some may be muddy in wet weather.

1. SP439198

Starting close to the church, walk down Church Street on the raised pathway, then continue down hill along Horse Shoe Lane towards the river.

Wootton was once the centre of an Anglo-Saxon royal estate: this included Old Woodstock, then a less important settlement. The name Wootton means "a settlement in a wood" and for centuries the parish was within the boundaries of the Royal Forest of Wychwood. Several of the farms in the parish originated as small hamlets situated in woodland clearings or assarts. The limestone soil of the area was difficult to cultivate so the hamlets declined during the Middle Ages and changed from arable cultivation to sheep farming. In modern times, the agricultural side of village life has declined again; most people do not work in the village but commute to large towns for employment.

Many of the village buildings are made of limestone, the older cottages fronting directly onto the road while the more modern buildings tend to be set back with gardens. Look at the stone walls and notice how the plants growing in the crevices are adapted to cope with very dry conditions. Stonecrop has succulent water-storing leaves while mosses can shut down their internal mechanisms to prevent water loss when very dry, and can use dew in the cool early morning to maintain essential processes.

Stonecrop

2. SP439196

Cross the bridge over the river Glyme and take the footpath to the left beside Bridge House. The path climbs steeply through a rocky gorge amongst shady trees. Through a small gate at the top, pause to look at the view of the Glyme valley and the village perched above it.

The low-lying meadows often flood, and it is not surprising that the settlement grew up on the hill top. Natural flooding deposits rich alluvium or river silt on the fields, so increasing fertility. During the 18th century, flooding was often engineered by making systems of channels and sluices. This allowed controlled winter flooding of water meadows which protected the grass from frost and led to an early crop for grazing or for mowing. These systems were often very elaborate, but the remnants of a simple form can be seen further along the route at Woodstock.

Climb the stile to the right alongside a garden. After a few yards cross the track and continue straight on in the same direction, keeping the hedge on your left.

This hedge contains several shrub species including hawthorn, field maple, elm, ash, elder and crab apple. This variety could indicate the hedge to be several hundred years old, or may be recent planting designed to be attractive to wildlife. The different flowers, fruits and seeds provide food at varying times for insects, birds and small mammals.

Follow the path in the same general direction as it leads through the hedge ahead.

Wayfaring tree

Guelder rose

Look at the surrounding landscape as you walk. The pattern of hills and valleys has influenced the development of land use over time. Small copses grow on steep-sided slopes which are more difficult to cultivate, whereas more gently sloping land is cultivated. These copses act as windbreaks and provide shelter for game birds and other animals.

The soil is full of lumps of limestone, broken up by centuries of ploughing. The presence of such stone shows that millions of years ago the area was underwater and formed the bed of a shallow sea (see Introduction).

Continue across the centre of a field and over a bank and stile, then alongside a fence with newly planted woodland on the right.

These two blocks of woodland contain a mixture of trees and shrubs. Two shrubs are closely related. Wayfaring tree (*Viburnum lanata*) grows only on calcareous (limy) soils and has downy leaves and berries which turn from red to black. Guelder rose (*Viburnum opulus*) has flat clusters of flowers, the outer ones much larger than the others. The berries are shiny red. This shrub is related to the garden variety known as "snowball bush" with round clusters of flowers, which is said to have originated from Guelderland in Holland, hence the name. These closely planted blocks of shrubs and trees act as valuable "islands" for animals to travel through the otherwise very open and exposed countryside.

3. SP442187

Eventually the path reaches a lane.

SHORT CUT
Turn left here and follow the lane over the bridge and uphill to cross the B4027. Continue along the track opposite to join the longer route at Point 7. Turn left to continue the walk.

Cross the lane and climb the steps up the bank opposite, continuing in the same direction. After a short distance look back to your left for a good view

Stratford bridge

of the bridge and the river. Continue on the same path across the fields to Woodstock.

The lane is called Stratford Lane and follows the route of the Roman Akeman Street from St Albans to Cirencester. The name Stratford is derived from the Old English word "straet" meaning Roman road. In turn this comes from the Latin *Via strata* – paved road. The earliest record of Stratford Bridge was in 1279 when it was repaired by the men of Hordley, one of the hamlets nearby which was closely linked to the royal estate. The villagers were allowed to take timber from nearby Wychwood Forest for this purpose. Today the Oxfordshire Way long distance footpath follows the line of Stratford Lane.

Both swallows and swifts are frequently seen in this valley during the summer. Swallows often search for their food by skimming low over the surface of rivers or ponds or under the canopy of tall widely spaced trees. Swifts fly much higher and are slightly larger birds, their swept-back wings making an aerodynamic silhouette. A different type of bird, which may also be seen or heard hereabouts, is the jackdaw, a small member of the crow family with a grey head. They are often associated with old buildings, nesting in chimneys and eaves, and come with rooks to feed on insects in the fields.

Jackdaw

The path passes close to Field Barn which marks the site of a shepherd's cottage, built in 1839 as a condition of a lease of Manor Farm in Old Woodstock.

The path itself is also an old route. Known as Wootton Way, it was declared a public road in 1770 when Wootton was inclosed. It is obviously not as much used now!

These open fields have been used for agriculture for many centuries. Pheasants, partridges and flocks of small finches may be seen as you walk. However, modern intensive cultivation has had a drastic effect on countryside birds. Autumn planting means that the crops are well grown in spring making it difficult for ground nesting birds to find bare soil for their nests. Lush growth often results in young birds getting very wet as they walk through dew-laden vegetation, so that they become very cold and may die. The early ripening of crops means that grain has been harvested before wild food sources become available in autumn, so that many birds die of starvation. Hence in recent years there has been a drastic decline in many rural bird populations including skylarks. However, set-aside land, with its wild grasses and plants being allowed to seed, may now encourage an increase in these bird and other animal populations.

Follow the path to the houses and onto a road. Turn right at Vermont Drive, then left when you reach the main road (A44).

4. SP441174

The route leads through Old Woodstock which was called "old" in 1294. The road itself has always been important, leading north to the Midlands. Now, much of the long-distance traffic has been diverted to the M40 but it is still busy so walk with care.

As you walk towards the town, notice the variety in building styles of the houses. Modern houses, like those just passed, tend to be very uniform in style and size, but older buildings, such as those along the main road, are more individual. Some were built to reflect the status of the inhabitants, a supreme example of this being Blenheim Palace.

If you cross the road close to a line of cottages on a raised roadway, you can take a short diversion into the grounds of Blenheim Palace.

The house and grounds were designed by Vanburgh in the early 18th century for the 1st Duke of Marlborough as a gift from the nation in recognition of his victories over the French. Later, in 1760 the grounds were "modernised" and landscaped by Capability Brown for the 4th Duke (see Introduction).

Continue further along the road, past the terrace of Victorian cottages built in 1870 to replace 16th century dwellings. Look out for a plaque marking the cottage where the Blenheim Orange apple first grew in the late 18th century. It was recommended as a cooking apple during the 19th century but now seems to have lost its popularity.

5. SP442169

At the bottom of the hill, on the left-hand side of the road, look out for steps down to a wooden walkway at the side of the bridge. Follow the walkway with the river on your left. Continue for some distance, past a sluice until you reach a kissing gate on the right.

This wet area to the right of the river Glyme is thought to have originated as a medieval fish pond. The river may have been dammed outside the Royal Park according to 13th and 14th century references. By the 16th century the area was known as the "Common Pool" and seems to have been let to tenants for four shillings (20p) with extra allowances to compensate for damage to the herbage caused by the horses of the King's servants. Although the area was divided into seven lots by drainage channels, some of which are still visible, it was not a true water-meadow (see Point 2).

The wet ground supports quite different vegetation to that seen elsewhere. There are patches of pink Himalayan Balsam, which was introduced to

Himalayan Balsam

31

*The River Glyme at
Woodstock*

British gardens from north India in about 1840. It was soon regarded as a garden weed and colonised river banks this century to become common in damp places. In late summer, the ripe seed pods open explosively to throw out their seeds, hence its successful colonisation. If you touch one end of a ripe seed pod, it will be enough to cause it to explode so leading to its other name of "Touch-me-not". The exploding seed pods operate by drying out along the seams where there are special thin-walled cells. These create high tension forces which rip the seed pod open.

In the river, other plants grow which prefer moving water. Water crowfoot can be seen with long flexible stems and submerged finely dissected leaves. The surface leaves are a different shape to those below the water. They are broader, similar to the related buttercup, and so much better able to use sunlight for photo-synthesis. The white flowers are held above the water surface to allow them to be pollinated by insects.

Many of the trees growing in this wet area are alders. The reddish-yellow male catkins can be seen in spring while the female flowers look like tiny pine cones, the old ones turning black. The roots and wood are resistant to rotting when wet, so was commonly used for making broom heads and clogs.

Water Crowfoot

Specialised insects may also be seen here whose

larvae live in water. Colourful damsel and dragon flies can easily be recognised, while stoneflies are small with two "tails" at the end of the body. Their larvae are often found clinging to stones, hence their name. Caddis flies have hairy wings which are held over the body like a roof. Their larvae live in the water in tubes which they construct of stones or plant stems, each type making their characteristic tube to protect them from the water current.

6. SP445170

Through the kissing gate, turn left at the first junction. Turn right at the next junction then over a bridge turn left. At the next junction turn left beside a bridleway sign. The road continues with a small industrial estate on the left and, further on, a cemetery on the right. The footpath continues in the same direction at the end of the road. Follow this for about a mile and a half or 2km.

Beyond the industrial estate the roadside verge is attractive. In early spring the sloe or blackthorn flowers well before the leaves are out and much earlier than hawthorn. The fruits are like small dark purple plums with a grey bloom caused by yeast growing on the surface. Such yeasts on other fruits, such as grapes, are essential in fermentation, turning the sugars to alcohol. Sloes are too bitter to eat but can be used in flavouring sloe gin or making jelly. Another plant which takes advantage of the early season is cow parsley. Although it does not flower until May, the leaves start sprouting in early winter. The plant is well grown by the spring and so able to out-compete other species for sunlight. The delicate creamy white flowers with finely dissected leaves are the earliest of a series of similar flowers belonging to the same family of umbellifers. During the summer the grass is regularly cut along these verges. This prevents long grasses and other plants from overgrowing the smaller flowers. Blue flowered bugle, cut-leaved geranium and hedge bedstraw all grow here.

The continuation of the road is now a footpath, known

as Dornford Lane. This is an ancient track dating probably from before the 10th century, and linked the demesne or Lord of the Manor's farm at Steeple Barton with the royal Anglo-Saxon manor 4.5 miles 7 km away at Woodstock. The farm produced supplies for the royal household and before the Norman Conquest was part of a seven thousand acre (over 3000ha) estate. Later the track was used by Welsh cattle drovers bringing their herds to the markets of southern England. Davis's map of Oxfordshire made in 1797 shows this track to be a well defined road, wider than it is today. It has a woodland feel to it now, as reduction in use has led to trees and shrubs encroaching from the hedgerow.

Pause for a moment at a gateway on the left to look at the view over the Glyme valley.

The river has formed a series of meanders further up the valley but nearby it seems to have been straightened. The Ordnance Survey map shows that the parish boundary follows the line of the old meanders although the water course is now straight.

You may see kestrels on the wing, searching for food

Kestrel

over the meadows bordering the river. Voles, mice, shrews, young rabbits, larger insects and worms are spied by the hovering bird which descends a short distance, and hovers again before finally diving onto its prey.

Along the track, notice the variety of climbing plants which scramble over the other vegetation. Traveller's joy or wild clematis is covered with creamy flowers in summer which mature into grey fluffy seed heads, each seed having a single long hairy plume which helps it to be blown away from the parent plant. The colour of the seed heads give rise to a third name – old man's beard. Two climbers both bearing poisonous red berries in autumn can be found. White bryony is related to the cucumber and has ivy-shaped leaves and tendrils, while black bryony is related to the tropical yam and has shiny heart-shaped leaves and no tendrils. Plants beside the track include ground ivy which unlike its namesake is not a climber. It has violet-blue flowers in spring and in the past was used to flavour and clarify beer before hops were substituted in the 18th century, as well as for herbal tea.

Ground ivy

At any time of the year, the small groups of black stalks and white powdery tips of the candle snuff fungus, resembling the base and wick of a candle, may be seen growing on the stumps and fallen stems of elder.

After a time the path widens, passing some hollows in the ground to the right, but you continue as before. Past a strip of pine trees, the path is open on the left. Cross the road with care and carry on along the track opposite.

The farm to the left along the road is Sansoms Farm and was the site of a toll house on the turnpike road between Wheatley and Glympton in the 18th century. Nearby, evidence has been found of a Roman farm dating from the 1st century AD which evolved into a villa over the following 300 years.

7. SP454191

After a time the track reaches a junction with a path. The SHORT CUT rejoins here by turning left onto the track.

This is Akeman Street again, a continuation of Stratford Lane which you crossed earlier.

The farm which can be seen across the fields to the left is Hordley Farm and is all that remains of the medieval hamlet whose men were required to maintain Stratford Bridge.

A DIVERSION can be taken here by turning right to follow the line of Akeman Street to the public house at Sturdy's Castle. Return to the main route by following a track to rejoin at Point 8 (see route map).

Along the path look out for dogwood in the hedgeline. This can be recognised by its red stems in winter and by its leaves with parallel veins in summer. If you carefully tear a leaf in half by breaking the veins, and then slowly draw apart the two halves, the thick, elastic sap forms threads which links them together. Many of the shrubs along the track grow from multiple stems, showing that in the past they have been regularly coppiced. This old management technique provided stakes and pliable poles for fence making and small repairs. The regular cutting would also have ensured that the path was kept clear of overgrowing vegetation and served to thicken the hedgeline.

8. SP456197

At a junction of paths, the track widens and after about 50 yards/metres, take the turning to the left.

Like Dornford Lane and Akeman Street it seems that this path was once more important than now, although its history is obscure.

As you walk notice the trees along the track. Many seem to have been planted for their ornamental value and are unusual in the wild. Look out for lime, walnut and larch in particular. You may also spot Midland or woodland hawthorn, with rounded rather than the lobed leaves of common hawthorn. Notice how some of the ash has been coppiced. Ash wood is light, strong and resilient and was used as handles for tools, shepherds' crooks and walking sticks, as well as more recently for sports equipment.

9. SP447197

The path emerges onto a farm track. Bear left, then right after a few yards/metres, down a narrow path which leads to the river. Follow the path to the bridge. Cross the bridge and take the road to the left, Milford Lane, which leads uphill back to Wootton.

Pause on Milford Bridge over the River Dorn and look at the meadow beside the water. In late spring, the pale pink flowers are ladies smock or cuckoo flower, so-called because it appears at about the same time as the cuckoo. The seed heads are eaten by the caterpillars of the orange tip butterfly, a relative of the cabbage white. The plant is a member of the cabbage family, the crushed leaves have the same smell because of chemicals called mustard oils. Insects are good botanists!

As you return to Wootton it is hard to believe that in the summer of 1872 the village was a centre of unrest amongst agricultural workers caused by poor housing and unemployment. They demanded a pay rise from 11 to 16 shillings (55p to 80p) a week. The employers turned down this demand and also formed an association to oppose the agricultural union movement. About 120 men were on strike during July and some union members left the area to seek work in Sheffield. With harvest approaching, the farmers took drastic measures and applied for soldiers to gather in the harvest. This was stopped by the Secretary of State for War and eventually most of the labourers returned to work, many with a pay rise.

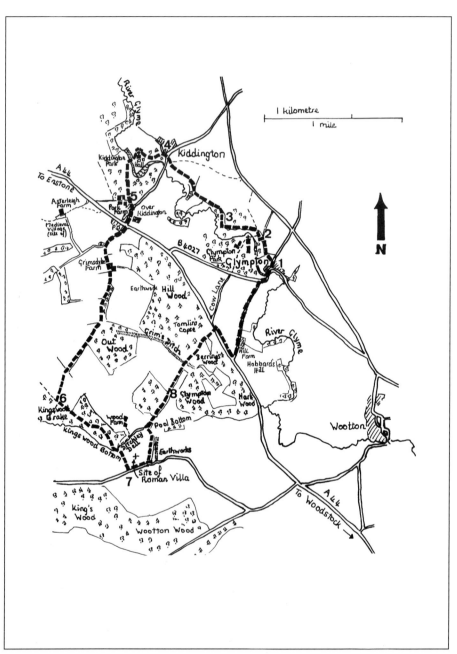

Key – see page 24.

Glympton & Kiddington

6.5 miles   10.5 km

This walk follows the Glyme valley for a short distance passing through the grounds of two country estates, before leading through ancient woodland containing evidence of medieval and earlier inhabitants.

1. SP427215

Start from the village hall at Glympton. Take the footpath beside the hall through the kissing gate, to a green gate. Follow the path along the top of a walled ditch, an overgrown ha-ha.

Glympton village at its present site is a relative newcomer. Previously it was situated close to the manor house and church, which you will see soon, but was moved to its present spot in the 17th century when the park was created around the house. Most of the present houses were built in the late 19th century; the almshouses are even more recent, dating from 1949, although designed in traditional style.

To the right as you walk across the first field, a line of large ash trees marks the fence line. The separate male and female flowers on the trees are produced before the leaves appear. The fertilised female flowers grow into large bunches of wind-dispersed winged seeds which are easily seen in winter. It takes a lot of energy to generate seeds and in some years, the trees produce no seeds as only male flowers appear.

The ha-ha which runs alongside the path on the left for some distance marks the edge of the formal grounds. Sunken boundaries act as barriers for animals and were favoured because they were hidden from view, so giving the spectator the impression that the grounds were larger than in reality.

Further along the path are many sycamore trees. Few types of insects feed on sycamores; most conspicuous is a species of green aphid. The winged adults space themselves carefully on the underside of the leaves as they do not like to touch each other. If disturbed, they produce an alarm odour which causes nearby aphids to jump off the leaf, so that a cloud of insects fly off together. In late summer, many black spots may be seen on the sycamore leaves. These are tar-spot fungus, which may weaken the tree and cause the leaves to fall early.

Horse chestnut trees

2. SP426219

Through the next gate, descend the steps to the road and turn left for about 30 yards/metres.

The house which can be seen is Glympton Park, the manor house. It was remodelled in the late 17th century, altered again in the 19th and is today undergoing further renovations. The park was first mentioned in 1665 and by 1759 the river had been dammed to form a serpentine lake, and a bridge and cascade constructed.

Take the path uphill on the right, leading into trees and eventually to the left of a fence. Continue through a gateway, then right through another gate into a large field, and continue in the same direction, keeping the fence on your left.

The large trees along the path are magnificent old specimens of horse chestnut. The deep shade of the trees keeps the ground beneath almost bare of plants. However, early in spring before the tree leaves are out, cow parsley and lords-and-ladies grow here. The large holes in the limbs of the trees may be favoured nest sites for all three types of British owls; barn, tawny and the smallest and most common day flying species, the little owl. Grey squirrels may be seen running up and down the trunks. This introduced species has replaced the

Little owl, Tawny owl, Barn owl

native red squirrel in many parts of Britain, although it is not certain that this is because of competition between the two; red squirrels were declining in places before grey squirrels appeared. The rotting dead wood is used for egg-laying by various wood boring beetles and numerous small holes can be seen where the adult beetles have emerged. Such old trunks are used by stag-beetle larvae which grow to 2-3 inches (6-7 cm) long. Like many other wood boring animals they are white as they do not need any special colouration for camouflage. Their heads are brown and hard and can be used to block a tunnel against predatory animals.

Past the trees, the fields are grazed by sheep and with the isolated specimen trees, there is a park-like feel to this area. Sheep keep the vegetation very short by biting the plants close to the ground whereas cattle pull plants with their lips and need taller herbage to eat. The close sheep grazing encourages a wide variety of plants to grow in the grass, all species which either grow flat or creep along the ground, so that they are difficult to nibble. However, plants protected by spines, prickles or a bitter taste, like thistles, nettles and docks, can become problems in grazed fields.

3. SP421221

Continue along the fence line until you reach a small white gate which leads into a wood. Through the gate, turn right and follow the path along the wood edge. At the far side of the wood, turn left and follow the path along the field edge, then straight across the field when the hedge turns sharp left. Continue in the same direction along a track beside a copse, then across the next field to reach a track which leads down to the road at Kiddington.

Along this stretch of the route is a pleasant view of the Glyme valley. The river here forms meanders in the flat valley, the line of the water marked by old pollarded willows. The rough vegetation on the valley slopes is full of nettles, thistles and other flowering plants. In the summer, the flowers are a rich source of nectar for butterflies and other insects, whilst in autumn and winter the seed heads are invaluable for finches and other birds and animals. The patches of woodland on both sides of the river appear on the 1st edition Ordnance Survey map made in the early 19th century. The age of the woodland is not known but its presence adds another habitat for wildlife as well as food and shelter. Visually the woodland adds variety to what would otherwise be an agricultural landscape.

As you walk over these fields, pause to look at the soil. It is full of stones and you will see that many contain fossils which have been formed in the limestone underlying this region of the county. You will find remains of shells which were laid down with other sediments in the warm shallow seas which covered this area during the mid-Jurassic period about 100 million years ago (see Introduction).

4. SP415229

In Kiddington, cross the road and go through the park gate beside the lodge. Follow the tarred track

Kiddington church

through ornamental trees past the church, where the footpath branches off to the left between box and laurel hedges to pass around the back of the church.

The mown lawns in the parkland clearly show the versatility of grass. Grasses grow from the base so cutting encourages them to branch and grow, thus ensuring good ground cover. Cereal crops are other types of grass which are grown for their "seeds", the grain, while hay contains grasses cut and dried to preserve the nutrients present before the seeds are produced.

The church of St Nicholas is in the Norman and Decorated styles but was restored in 1879. The churchyard is a quiet haven for many types of wild life. Wild flowers can grow undisturbed amongst the graves, thus encouraging insects to feed, and in their turn, birds and small mammals which feed on the insects. Mosses and lichens grow on the gravestones. These slow growing plants utilise crevices and depressions on rough stone to gather scarce nutrients and water. Lichens are a mixture of fungus and alga growing intimately intermixed, each helping the other to gain food and moisture.

Continue past a stone dovecote and down a grassy slope to the lake and the river. Over the footbridge, follow the path up hill, where good views of the house and gardens can be seen, and continue to the road.

Kiddington Hall, surrounded by a walled park, was remodelled in about 1850, incorporating a house built in 1673. In 1739 Lancelot "Capability" Brown redesigned the park, probably his first contract in Oxfordshire. The river was dammed to form a sinuous lake and specimen trees planted. The ornamental flower beds or parterres on the terrace were laid out in 1850 in keeping with the house which was remodelled then in an Italianate style.

Along the waterside you may see Canada geese. These decorative introduced birds have settled and bred so well in this country that in some places they are now considered a pest. They graze on short grass and may therefore either create a mess with droppings in parks or else eat young crops in farmland. The species is

Stone dovecote

widely distributed worldwide, and apart from slight colour variations, also varies in size; the British birds are some of the largest types.

5. SP411223

At the road, turn right and walk to the main road. Cross with care and continue straight on down a lane. At the junction bear left and follow the track uphill, past Grimsdyke Farm and then alongside a copse on the left until you reach woodland.

Amongst the plants in the hedgerows bordering the lane, look for the striking small purple and yellow flowers of woody nightshade or bittersweet. This climber is often confused with the rarer deadly nightshade which belongs to the same family, *Solanaceae*. Some members of this plant group contain chemicals which are poisonous but which are also used in medicine. Atropine, for example, made from deadly nightshade, is a heart drug and also dilates the pupils of the eyes. Its Latin name of *belladonna* meaning "beautiful lady" stems from the Roman practice of dilating the pupils to enhance the appearance. Many Roman women must have had blurred vision as a result! Other members of this family include potato, tomato, sweet pepper and aubergine, used as food plants, while tobacco is utilised for its drug, nicotine.

At the woodland, go right through a gate and follow the woodland edge with the trees on your left.

Deadly nightshade

Woody nightshade

Out Wood, passed on the left, is an old wood, recorded in a survey of the eastern woodlands of Wychwood Forest, ordered by James I in 1609. Look through the trees to see bluebells in the spring. Dog's mercury also grows here, visible early in the year as fresh green shoots, long before most other plants are growing. You will also see many hazel bushes, coppiced in the past to produce a regular supply of long pliable poles which had many uses around the farm.

Continue along this track after it leaves the woodland for just over 0.5 miles, 1km, keeping the fence on your left.

Continue on through a thick hedge line, and bear slightly left across a large field towards a belt of trees.

The thick hedge which the track passes through marks the line of the parish boundary between Enstone and Kiddington. It contains many different tree and shrub species which indicates its great age.

6. SP401202

Turn left on the track alongside the conifer tree belt and follow the track through woodland. Over a small bridge, the track joins a lane. Go to the right, uphill to the road.

This wood is another old one called Kingswood Brake. Although there has been conifer planting, there are many plants which indicate ancient woodland; woodruff, with tiny white flowers and whorls of leaves around the stalk, wood millet, a delicate grass, primroses and wood spurge with stiff greenish flowerheads which slowly turn brown over the year and remain on the plant through the winter. Common spotted orchids grow along the track. Notice how the stalk bearing each flower is twisted so that the flower is held upside down. In spring the greenish sheaths of lords and ladies or wild arum can be seen. Each flower has a tall spike in the centre which generates heat from the breakdown of tissues and produces a smell like rotting meat which attracts small flies. They enter the flower but are trapped by hairs at the base. Here the flies pollinate the flower and are

49

Fallow deer

released within 24 hours when the hairs wither. In autumn the spikes of bright orange fleshy seeds are eaten by snails and birds, so distributing the seeds.

Look out for animal prints in the soft mud along the path. You may spot the two-toed mark of the fallow deer, which if you are quiet, you may see grazing. The bucks can be recognised by their flattened antlers, shaped like the fingers of a hand, together with a vertical white stripe on either side of their rump. These deer are native to the east Mediterranean and may have been introduced into Britain by the Romans.

Along the path, especially after rain you may find the so-called Roman or edible snail, our largest snail. These are rare creatures and must not be destroyed or removed.

Roman snail

Grim's Ditch

It is unlikely that the Romans actually introduced them to this country, although the inhabitants of the nearby Roman villa may well have eaten them.

7. SP409194

At the road, turn left and walk with care for 200 yards/metres to a bridleway sign on the left. Follow this path downhill with the hedge to the right.

Where the path turns left into the field off the road, look to your right into the next field and unless the crop is very high you will notice a raised bank running parallel to the path. This may date from the 1st century AD and links with Grim's Ditch, a large system of earth works in this part of west Oxfordshire. In another nearby field, a Roman villa was found earlier this century with a painted floor which unfortunately was destroyed. It appears to have been occupied from the 1st to the 4th centuries AD, and other finds suggest the site was inhabited long before the Romans built there.

At the end of the field, go down the bank on the right and continue downhill between two banks with a field edge on the right.

The banks on each side of the path mark the parish boundary between Stonesfield and Glympton. The line of the hedge and boundary is shown on a map dating from 1797 but the boundary dates back to Saxon times if not earlier.

Elder bushes are conspicuous in this scrubby woodland. The seeds are usually dispersed in bird droppings, hence the common occurrence of these bushes along hedgelines where birds may perch. Rabbits don't like the taste of elder so these shrubs tend to grow unhindered by any grazing. The stems of the shrub often have very soft, flattened rubbery fungus on them known as "Jew's ears", after the story that Judas Iscariot hanged himself from an elder tree. The fungus is edible with a pleasant nutty flavour. The wood floor is carpeted with moss. These are primitive plants and have no specialised internal tissues for conducting water and chemicals within the plant. The leaves form a series of overlapping structures around the stem so that water can move up the plant on the outside through these fine channels. Mosses are very dependent on water for their reproduction hence most are found in moist shady places. In many places the moss has been pulled up and scattered about by blackbirds and other birds searching for food.

The path crosses a stream and then goes through a gate into a field. Turn right here and continue to another small gate leading into woodland. Keep close to the woodland edge on the right as the path leads downhill to a clearing and then uphill in the same direction, passing a large specimen sycamore tree on the left-hand side.

The woodland contains many large cherry trees, which bear white flowers in the spring. They can be identified by the bark which is often shiny and patterned with horizonal stripes. The woodland is not dense, even though some conifers have been planted. The light shade allows many plants to thrive on the woodland floor, unlike darker woods which tend to have bare ground beneath the trees.

8. SP414203

At the end of the wood, keep straight on through a gate and continue in the same direction with a hedge on the right and then on into more woodland, bearing left as you enter the trees.

Not far into this woodland area, Berring's Wood, just past a junction of tracks, notice a wide ditch and bank which cross the line of the track. This is another section of Grim's Ditch which roughly encircles an area of 22 square miles in this part of Oxfordshire. The earthworks are thought to have been constructed during the late Iron Age, just prior to the Roman occupation of the area. The neighbouring estate of Ditchley is thought to have been named after this earthwork, its name meaning "the woodland clearing beside the ditch".

Other earthworks, elsewhere in this wood, mark the remains of a hamlet known as Boriens, from which the present name of the wood is likely to be derived. It was first recorded in 1246 and had four households in 1279 when it belonged to Kiddington manor. However, people from Glympton also lived there and later it seems to have been part of Glympton manor. It was depopulated in the late 14th century but 600 years later traces of house platforms and stone foundations can still be found beside the ruins of a 19th century keeper's cottage.

Continue along the main track. Past the cottage, the track starts to climb. Look out for a path on the left. Follow this uphill to emerge through a gate on to the main A44 road. Turn right and walk with care for about 500m to the turning for Glympton. Follow this minor road back to the village, turning right at the junction and back to the start.

At the entrance to Glympton village, pause on the bridge. The River Glyme flows over a weir which holds back the water forming the lake within Glympton Park. Further along the formalised river are some old wooden stocks, a former punishment for village wrong doers.

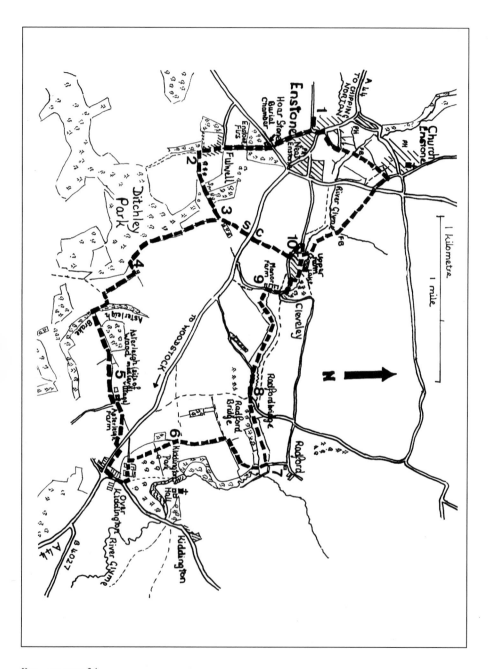

Key – see page 24.

WALK 3

Enstone and Ditchley

7.5 miles   12 km

Short cut 3 miles   5 km

This walk leads through several quiet hamlets and part of the Ditchley estate, returning to Enstone along the secluded valley of the River Glyme. There are wide-ranging views to be seen on clear days.

1. SP376241

Start from the youth hall car park in Enstone. Coming out of the entrance, turn left, then right and walk along the road to a junction.

One of the most obvious features of this landscape is the use of stone for building. The old cottages and the stone walls lining the road are built of Cotswold or Oolitic limestone. The art of stone walling is dying out in many places and walls are being replaced by wire fences which can be moved quite easily for flexible land use. Recently, grants to farmers have encouraged the planting of trees and hedges, so in time, the character of this landscape may change from an open, spacious countryside to one which is more enclosed and shady. One disadvantage of such an open landscape is the difficulty in siting large buildings sympathetically. The structure on the skyline to the left is a grain silo, used by local farmers. It is controversial as it is visible for miles around.

The verge alongside the walls contains many wild flowers. A characteristic plant of this area is meadow cranesbill with bright blue flowers throughout the summer. There are several members of this plant family, all with long pointed seed pods, which give rise to the name of "cranesbill".

At the junction carry straight on downhill, walking through the hamlet of Fulwell.

Just past the cross roads, look out on the right for a small enclosure which contains the remains of a dolmen or burial chamber, which may date from the Megalithic period, earlier than the Neolithic. The huge standing stone, known as the Hoar Stone, would have been part of the side wall which supported a capstone as a roof. The broken remains of the other stones lie close by. The whole structure was covered with earth which has since eroded away but its size means that, like the grain silo, it would have been visible over a wide area.

The road leads through woodland planted in the 1950's known as Enstone Firs. It now contains sycamore

Hoar stone

Biddy's Bottom cottage

and ash as well as Scots pine, larch and spruce. Ash has black leaf buds and leaves divided into several leaflets. It is often the last to come into leaf in the spring and the first to drop its leaves in the autumn. The leaves do not change colour before they fall and so maximise their efficiency in photosynthesis to make up for their relatively short existence. Both ash and sycamore colonise quite rapidly, as the seeds are carried in the wind, although here it is not certain whether they were planted or arrived on their own. Look out for red flowered woundwort along the road side, so-called because the leaf extracts have antiseptic properties. "Wort" was the medieval name for herbaceous plants.

Fulwell is one of the seven hamlets of Enstone and has changed little over the years. The last cottage on the right, called Biddy's Bottom, was the home of Mont Abbott whose life story as a local farm labourer and shepherd is told in the book "Lifting the Latch" by Sheila Stewart. Look out for the old oven built into the wall on the side of one of the cottages.

2. SP379230

Through the hamlet, take the footpath to the left through a gate and follow it along the field edge.

In the field, the slope to the left shows conspicuous hollows and bumps. There are similar sites elsewhere in the hamlet, all of which represent the remains of cottages, indicating that Fulwell was once a much larger settlement.

The Ist Edition Ordnance Survey map, published in 1830, shows that the path from Fulwell was a more important route in the past. Now all that is left is a footpath along a raised causeway which indicates the line of the old lane. It is edged with old rotting elm stumps which have been replaced with a line of horse chestnuts. English elms were a feature of the rural landscape until they were decimated by Dutch elm disease in the 1970's. This widespread loss occurred because elms reproduce from root suckers rather than seed, so that all elms are very similar genetically. This meant that they are all susceptible to the disease, and no individuals have any resistance to it. Look at these stumps and others further along the path to see a wide variety of fungi and algae growing on the wood. Only the fruiting parts are visible as "toadstools", the main structure exists as fine threads throughout the tree stump, digesting the wood through enzyme action.

Through the gate carry straight on down the valley and over the stile at the end. Continue along the field edge, looking out for a path off to the right after 100 yards/metres.

In wet weather a spring may be gushing from the ground close to the gateway. It may be this which gave the hamlet its name, Fulwell meaning "foul spring".

3. SP385233

(For a SHORT CUT, continue straight on here. Follow the path to the left of the plantation ahead and continue to the road. Cross over and follow the path ahead to Cleveley. At the road, turn left for about 300 yards/ metres. At a junction, turn right to reach a path close

to a large pond. Here turn left, rejoining the main walk at Point 10.)

The path leads off to the right through a gap in the hedge, going uphill with the hedge on the left.

The soil in this area is quite stony and is known as stonebrash. Sometimes you may find a shell or coral fossil as this type of rock was formed from deposits laid down in the sea during the Jurassic Period (see Introduction).

Continue straight on through a patch of trees, then turn left and right outside the wood edge. Continue along this track for about half a mile or 1km.

The woodland edge follows the line of the parish boundary between Spelsbury and Kiddington, although here there is no physical evidence to be seen (see Section 4). The woodland on the right has been planted in blocks, on the site of an ancient wood. The field to the left was named Winchcombe Assarts on a map made by Edward Grantham in 1726. This name refers to the clearing of woodland for sheep pasture in the Middle Ages by the Abbey of Winchcombe in Gloucestershire which held Enstone from the time of the Domesday Book.

Along the wood edge is a band of natural vegetation with plants like bracken, bramble and traveller's joy. Another attractive plant to be seen is another "wort". Perforate St John's Wort has yellow flowers with small black dots on the edge of the petals. When held up to the light, the leaves reveal translucent dots. These contain minute oil droplets which give off an aromatic smell when the leaves are crushed. This plant has been introduced to Australia and the USA where it has spread extensively through over-grazed pastures to become a troublesome weed.

In summer several types of brown butterfly can be seen here. Ringlets are very dark with large circular marks called eye-spots on their underwings. Meadow browns are larger and paler and prefer the open grassy areas to the woodland edge. Similar to the last, but smaller with bright orange patches on the wings is the hedge brown. All these butterflies need flowers like

59

thistles and brambles as nectar sources, while their caterpillars feed on grasses. Hence they live on wide field edges or roadside verges which provide the right conditions for all stages of their life cycle.

4. SP391220

Level with a stone building, turn left towards it along a track. Follow the path past the building to the right and continue with the hedge on your left along the field edge.

The track and fields are shown on the 1726 map. The hedge bordering the track to the left contains a good mixture of species including field maple, hazel, hawthorn, sloe, wayfaring tree and elder. This variety provides a rich food source in flowers and berries for birds, small mammals and insects. The hedge may be an old one, derived from woodland clearance, but may alternatively have been planted with these species relatively recently (see Introduction).

At a junction of tracks close to a large barn, turn left following the hedgeline. At the woodland edge the path turns right.

Close to the junction, there are views to the right towards Ditchley Park and House. This is an ancient estate with its roots at least in the Roman period when there was a villa there. From here not much can be seen of the house and park but the large, isolated, specimen trees indicate the landscaped grounds which were designed by Capability Brown in the 1770's. The present house was rebuilt in 1720 by James Gibbs for the 2nd Earl of Lichfield, replacing the earlier house purchased by his ancestor, Sir Henry Lee, in 1583.

After about 150 yards/metres (close to large trees), look for a path leading through the woodland. Take the path over a bank through the woodland strip.

The strip of woodland is called Asterleigh Brake. Notice that many of the species at the woodland edge are the same as those found in the rich hedge seen earlier. The obvious bank marks the line of the parish boundary between Enstone and Kiddington.

Turn right out of the trees through a gate into a field where you walk with the hedge on the left. Continue in the same direction past a wood and onto a track leading to a farm.

The area of woodland further along the path is called Asterleigh Wood, the name marking the approximate site of the medieval village of Asterleigh. This was a hamlet in the parish of Over Kiddington and was probably linked with it in the Domesday Book. There were fewer than ten households in 1428 and by 1466 the village was abandoned. It may have declined due to the Black Death or as a result of inclosure of land for sheep pasture.

Once past the woodland, the landscape reverts to the open landscape seen earlier. The wooded landscape around Ditchley reflects the old area of Royal Forest which existed here for many centuries. It also demonstrates the effect of large family-owned estates which can absorb the long-term land use of woodland and plantations bringing little immediate profit. Smaller land owners need to use the land differently for the quick profit to be had in food production.

5. SP400222

Walk past Asterleigh Farm, turning left at a junction of tracks. Follow this track turning right beside farm buildings, then after 100yards/metres go over a stile on the right, taking the footpath bearing left across fields. Go through a gateway and past a patch of trees through a gate to the road.

At Asterleigh Farm, notice the small plantation of trees on the site of a disused quarry. Two of the species get their names from the appearance of their leaves. Whitebeam has a felty-white underside to its leaves and mountain ash resembles ash with several leaflets arranged on a stem. Other planted trees include cherry, maple and field maple. Field maple is the only native maple in Britain; the other maples and sycamore have been introduced during the last few hundred years.

Both this farm and Park Farm further along the walk are good habitats for many birds. Martins and swallows,

Mountain ash

which migrate to England in the summer, can be seen catching insects in the air. Martins have white breasts and short, broad forked tails; swallows have dark backs with long slender forked tails. Muddy patches provide material for nests which are tucked against the eaves outside or inside the farm buildings. Other birds like wagtails, robins, chaffinches and sparrows can also be seen, all attracted by food in the form of insects and grain.

At the road turn right and walk on the pavement to the crossroads where you take the lane on the left to Over Kiddington, crossing with care. Continue past the cottages to the track leading off to the left beside an old stone cross. Follow this track for 100 yards/metres before turning left through Park Farm yard. Bear to the left through the yard to emerge on a track. After 50 yards/metres take the stile on the right and follow the track for some distance.

Past Park Farm, the route leads between two very different landscapes. To the left is improved grassland, grazed by animals or cut for silage, while to the right is the parkland of Kiddington Hall. Parkland like this was designed to emulate an idealised natural landscape with undulating hills, groups of trees and sinuous waterways, all carefully placed to be viewed to its best from the house. It was also a means of impressing the neighbours! This park was designed by Capability Brown and is thought to have been his first Oxfordshire contract in about 1739. The spreading specimen trees are typical of parkland; the distinctive flat base of the foliage occurs due to animal grazing. There are good views from here of the house, gardens and river which can be seen close up in Walk 2.

There are few wild flowers along the track because of the fertilizers which are used on the adjacent fields. Fertilizer encourages the growth of vigorous grasses and plants like clover at the expense of smaller flowering plants. However, several species of thistle grow beside the path. Large woolly thistle flowers have a delicate framework of long threadlike

Woolly thistle

Kiddington Hall

hairs, hence the name. Spear thistles are upright, without the long hairs and creeping thistles have much smaller flowers. Bees and butterflies are attracted to the flowers but the prickly leaves are avoided by grazing animals. The leaves may be attacked by small flies whose larvae mine tunnels inside the leaf, eating the tissue. Living inside the prickly leaf serves as good protection for these insects from many predators.

6. SP407229

As the track starts to climb uphill, the path leaves it, goes through a gate on the left and continues in the same direction on the other side of the wall. Continue in this direction until you reach a hedge in front of you. Go through the gap and turn right.

The thick field hedge on your right marks another part of the parish boundary between Enstone and Kiddington. It contains elm (with "wings" on the bark), hazel, elder, hawthorn and sloe. It is likely to be very old and is a considerable feature, although modern hedge flailing, rather than laying, will tend to thin the hedge rather than rejuvenate it. In places notice the bank on which the hedge grows, indicating its age and importance. **Continue in the same direction into the next field almost to the corner where the path leaves the hedgeline and heads diagonally left for the cottage in the valley. At the cottage, take the path to the right past the side of the house and down to a lane.**

Close to the cottage, the path reaches the river valley. The ground is much wetter here and the plants reflect this with creamy meadowsweet, collected in the past because of its pleasant smell for strewing on the floor, and great willow herb with large pink flowers.

The cottage is actually Radford Mill, which was mentioned in the Domesday Book in 1086. Upstream, the water course has been engineered to make full use of the water power.

7. SP409237

Over the small bridge, cross the stile to the left and take the footpath up the valley parallel with the river. After less than 0.5mile/ 0.75km, you will reach a road.

This quiet valley is grazed by cattle but the wet areas close to the river contain wet-loving species like meadowsweet, burr reed, *Juncus* rushes and spindly, dark-flowered marsh thistle. The clumps of rush leaves are really modified stems, as shown by the clusters of brown flowers on some of them. The bank to the right is too steep for cattle to graze heavily, and numerous wild flowers grow here. Scabious, trefoil, clover, bird's foot trefoil and many others grow here that are absent elsewhere in the field. Large, hawker dragonflies sweep over the vegetation; the males set up territories and chase away other males in the hope of finding a female. They also hunt in these areas, using their legs to catch other insects as they fly by and then settling on a prominent perch to eat their prey.

Where the path is close to the river you can find water cress growing. It has four petalled, white flowers and the leaves smell of cabbage when crushed. This plant, not surprisingly, belongs to the cabbage family, unlike fool's water cress with which it is sometimes confused. The latter has similar leaves but the flowers are in clusters or umbels, the leaves smell very unpleasant and the plant belongs to the carrot family.

8. SP403236

Turn left onto the road, over Radford Bridge, and continue towards Cleveley. The river is on your right. As the road bends away from the river, continue straight on, taking the path through the gateway into a field. Follow the river for about 0.5 miles/ 0.75km, passing through another gate on the way. After the path leaves the river, take the stile to the right, about 100 yards/metres past a metal gate. Cross this field to the stile at the far end which leads onto the road.

As you walk along the road and the path beyond, the river is lined with neatly pollarded willows. This traditional management prevents old heavy branches

Pollarded willows beside the Glyme

from splitting and falling off. On closer inspection these trees will reveal some surprises. The crowns of the trunks accumulate decomposing leaf litter which makes a good bedding compost for wind or bird deposited seeds. See how many different plants have colonised these tree tops.

In the fields on the valley slopes to the left, particularly past the metal gate, the grassland is very different to that seen at Kiddington, for example. It has not been improved with fertilizers and is rich in flowering plants. It is officially classed as "unimproved calcareous grassland" and it is known that this slope has not been ploughed for at least a hundred years and probably never sprayed with pesticides. This type of grassland may now be awarded an Environmentally Sensitive Area payment to encourage the farmer to retain the traditional management in order to conserve this flora and fauna. Amongst the flowers to be seen here are scabious, pink restharrow and pyramidal orchids, dwarf thistle, and yellow bird's foot trefoil and agrimony. Purging flax, with tiny white star-shaped flowers, is related to the blue flowered linseed which is becoming common as an oil producing crop in this area.

The final field shows a pattern of ridge-and-furrow, not seen anywhere else on this route. This indicates that this field (and probably others not crossed by public

Rest harrow

footpaths) were taken out of arable cultivation, possibly in the 14th or 15th century, and have remained as grassland ever since.

9. SP391237

Turn right along the road and continue uphill into Cleveley past cottages and more modern houses. Look out for a footpath sign on the right. Follow the track which leads downhill back to the river bank. Turn left along the river.

The old cottages in Cleveley again show the traditional local use of stone, whereas the modern dwellings tend to use materials which are now cheaper and easier to use. Notice the old barn which has been converted into a house. This use of redundant farm buildings preserves the appearance of a settlement, even if the old way of life has disappeared.

The banks on each side of the road contain some attractive wild flowers. Bright yellow clusters of tiny flowers belong to ladies bedstraw. The title "ladies" in flower names often refers to Mary, "Our Lady". This plant has a traditional connotation with the Nativity, the story being that the fine leaves and flowers were used as bedding for the crib.

The path down to the river is an old route, shown by the steep banks on each side. The ground has been gradually eroded away due to the passage of feet and hooves and the action of rainwater flowing downhill.

Along the river bank look out for stoneflies, with two pairs of wings and two long tails, and for caddis flies with hairy wings, making them look like small slim moths. Both insects spend most of their lives, one or two years, as aquatic larvae. The adult stage is often quite short lived; the insects do not feed and their main function is to disperse the species, flying to another site to reproduce.

The shady conditions along the path induce spindly growth and thin leaves in plants which are more substantial if growing in the open. Nettles and hogweed are examples of this. Cow parsley and violets flower in the spring before the leaves on the trees cast a deep shade over the path.

At more cottages turn right, following a bridleway sign past the large pond.

The SHORT CUT rejoins the main trail.

The large pond in the village contains a variety of domestic and semi-domestic waterfowl. Mute swans, grey lag geese, canada geese, mallards with curly feathers near the tail, green winged small teal and tall "runner" ducks can all be seen here. The different sizes of birds and the length of their necks enable them to use different types of food, so reducing competition for resources. Geese often feed on grass at the side of the water. Ducks feed in the shallows but swans, with their long necks, can reach deep underwater to pull weed from the bottom.

10. SP389241

Past the pond in front of Upper Farm bear left uphill between stone walls. Cross over a plank footbridge after about 300 yards/metres, then walk uphill along a grassy track to emerge on to a road. Cross the road with care and continue straight on.

The grassy route from Cleveley to Enstone is another which is shown on old maps to be more important than

Wild liquorice

now. The hedge bordering the first section contains coppiced hazel, field maple, sloe, plum and elder. Hops also grow in the hedge; surprisingly this plant is related to elm and to stinging nettles.

The stream crossed by the plank bridge arises from a spring further up the valley. There are many springs in this area and no shortage of running water. This is reflected in some of the place names like Fulwell and Radford with others, like Chalford, further away. Springs arise where the geology changes from porous limestone to impervious rock or clay. If the level of the water table remains constant, then the flow from such springs is often more reliable than in rivers which may depend on much of their flow from rainwater. The erosive action of quite small streams like this one can cause a valley to develop over many thousand years.

Along the grassy "green" track, amongst the commoner purple knapweed or hardheads, look for wild liquorice, a plant which is not widespread. The characteristic shape of the greenish cream flowers show that it is a member of the pea or vetch family. It is related to the cultivated plant grown for flavouring and sweets.

At the top of the track, the hedge is planted with cypress. This exotic (ie non-native) tree is the food plant of the caterpillar of a continental moth, Blair's shoulder knot; its extensive planting in gardens has allowed the moth to spread throughout southern Britain.

Look for a path to the left. Go downhill to the next stile and continue to the steps onto a footbridge over the river. Follow the walkway and path over stiles, and continue straight on uphill to emerge on to a back street of Enstone. Turn left and follow the road to the main road where you turn left again. Cross with extreme care, then turn right twice to return to the village hall car park.

The views over Enstone show that the village is mostly spread over the dry hill tops and, when you reach the marshy river valley, the reason for this is apparent. Settlements invariably grew up where there was a good water supply but were situated where there was no danger of flooding.

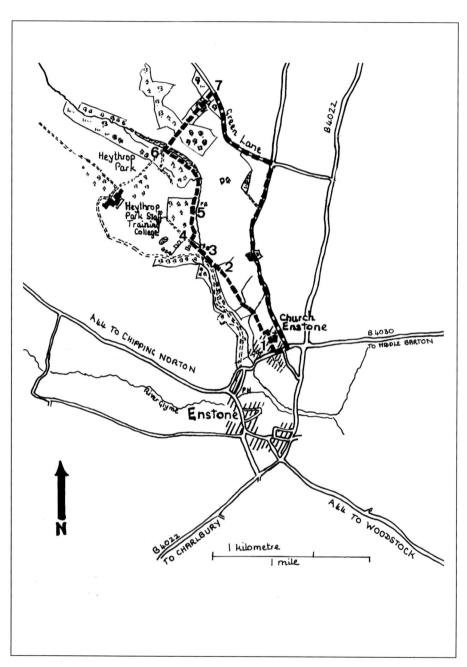

Key – see page 24.

Heythrop

4.5 miles   7 km

This is a short walk from Church Enstone through part of the landscaped grounds of Heythrop House, returning via a quiet country road.

1. SP380251

Start from the lych gate of St Kenelm's church in Church Enstone, taking the path to the left of the churchyard.

Both the church and grave yard are worth pausing to look at. The churchyard has much potential nature conservation value as areas of longer grass and wildflowers are being left to grow naturally, rather than all being close-mown. The holly bush growing here shows a rather characteristic feature of its growth. The leaves on the lower part of the tree are very prickly, whereas those towards the top lack the sharp spines. It is thought that this reflects the value of protection of the lower leaves against damage from browsing animals such as deer; the upper leaves are out of reach and so do not need such protection.

At the junction of paths bear left. Go straight on through a gateway (which may be latched) to a stile and turn left down a track.

The verge on the right of the track has been planted with shrubs including viburnum and buddleia. Although not a native species, buddleia is very attractive to

*Decorated doorway,
St. Kenelm's Church*

wildlife, the flower spikes providing a rich nectar source for butterflies and other insects and the seedheads a source of food for finches.

After 50yards/metres at a left bend in the track, turn right along the field edge with a hedge on your left. Over the stile, continue straight on across the next field, over another stile, then bear diagonally left across the next field to a third stile.

As you walk through the first field, notice the plantation of "Christmas" trees or Norway spruce. Such planting is an alternative cash crop for farmers but at the same time offers cover for game birds and other animals, as well as an area which will not be disturbed for some years.

2. SP375258

Over the stile, the path bears to the left going down hill and then climbs again before dropping to a stile in the left far corner of the field. Here the path crosses a stream over stepping stones and bears right as directed by the sign.

The fields crossed earlier have all been "improved" with fertilizer or pesticides but this rougher pasture is rather different. Where the path descends into a small steep valley and climbs again, look carefully at the ground to see the variety of plants growing here. The valley bottom is poorly drained and tussocks of a tough leaved grass, *Deschampsia*, common hair grass, indicate this.

Three quite uncommon plants to be found are lady's mantle, with greenish yellow flowers and pleated leaves, and dropwort with creamy white flowers similar to meadow sweet. A third, betony with deep pink flowers, is related to deadnettle and like the other species prefers grassy habitats. These plants are uncommon now because most grassland has been treated and either the grasses out-grow the flowering plants, or the non-grasses are killed. The cattle grazing here churn up or poach the soft ground and this can be beneficial to the plants because it reduces the chances of large and vigorously growing plants out-competing other species. Open ground for seeds is also beneficial for plants which may otherwise not be able to spread.

At the top of the slope are maple trees which offer shade and shelter for cattle. The animals enjoy eating the foliage; notice how the lower branches have been eaten producing a level flat appearance known as the browse line.

Plants at the stream edge again reflect the different water requirements and tolerances of various species.

At the water's edge grows blue flowered brooklime and white flowered watercress. The unrelated fool's watercress also grows here but it is not edible. On the slightly drier banks look for pink ragged robin, yellow flags and bushes of white flowering guelder rose.

Pause and look for numerous wolf spiders roving over the ground. They do not make webs but are active hunters, often ambushing small insects. In spring the females carry their silk wrapped eggballs around with them, supported by their back legs. When the eggs hatch, the young spiders are carried on the mothers' backs until they soon wander off on their own.

3. SP372259

Continue beneath the electricity cables heading uphill towards the electricity pole to emerge on a carpark. Immediately, take the path on the right, following it left beside the hedge then turning right again at the sign into woodland.

The grassland beyond the stream shows what happens when the vegetation is not regularly grazed. A rich mixture of buttercups, ragged robin and a host of other flowers grow here. The absence of many nettles and large grass tussocks would indicate that the vegetation is cut regularly but it is obvious how this activity results in quite a different collection of plants compared with the cattle grazed areas.

4. SP371261

The path leads through woodland and after about a quarter of a mile or 0.5 km it descends to the right to the stream.

There are several different types of conifers in the woodland. See how many you can spot. Yews have broad soft needles with a prominent midrib on the upper side. Pines have clusters of needles while those of firs arise singly from the twigs. The pines often have trickles of thick sticky resin running down the trunks. This is good protection against insects and fungi if the tree is damaged. The resin of some species actually contain a hormone compound very similar to one produced by insects called "juvenile hormone". This is important in insects ensuring proper growth and development. However, if present in excess, if eaten from a plant, it can cause deformities and prevent proper development. Hence this is a natural insecticide which is used in some artificial control products produced by chemical manufacturers. The sticky resin often traps insects. Over a long period of time, the resin may be fossilised and turned to amber; fossil hunters occasionally find the insects preserved inside.

A plant to look for in the summer is enchanter's nightshade with delicate white flowers. Its fruits are covered in small bristles which catch on to the coats of animals so dispersing the seed over a wide area. The "magic" connotations of the plant's name date back to at least Roman times.

The fruiting bodies of several types of fungi may be seen growing on fallen timber in this woodland. Whitish leathery brackets of the birch polypore are only found on this type of tree. The name comes from the tube-like pores lined with spores arising from its lower surface. Another, *Daldinia concentrica* belongs to another group of fungi, forming spherical black fruiting bodies with the consistency of charcoal. The Latin name refers to the concentric lines seen when the fungus is cut open, while its English names of cramp balls or King Alfred's cakes refer to a belief in its use in relieving cramp and the historical legend of the burnt cakes respectively.

Notice how some of the trees arise from multiple trunks. This reflects the old management practice of coppicing trees. Most species can be coppiced by cutting them down to ground level when they will then grow up again from the cut trunk. The practice produces poles which were used in the past for different purposes depending on the types of wood, its size, colour and hardness. Coppicing also extends the life of a tree as it encourages new growth and reduces the chances of rot and damage which normally occurs on larger older trunks.

Summerhouse, Heythrop Park

5. SP372264

**Continue along the water side for another half mile
or just less than 1km until a tarred estate road is
reached.**

The series of pools and waterfalls along the valley
are obviously artificial. Heythrop House and Park were
constructed in the early part of the 18th century. The
estate was bought by Charles Talbot, the Earl of
Shrewsbury, in 1697. He was an eminent statesman of
the period and was involved in the invitation to William
of Orange to become King of England in 1688. Talbot
travelled widely on the continent and was influenced by
classical architecture. He commissioned Thomas Archer
to design the house and probably the grounds which were
completed in 1716. At this time these grounds were
considered to be quite innovative, with winding walks
through groves of trees, a contrast to the more formal
lay-out more usually found in England at that time. The
house was gutted by fire in 1831, but restored 40 years

later by Albert Brassey, the son of Thomas, a great
railway builder. In the 1920's the estate was divided into
three and the house and over 400 acres was bought by
the Jesuits who used it as a college. In 1969 the property
was sold to the National Westminster bank as a training
and conference centre.

The varying conditions provided by the different
sections of the water course provide habitats for a variety
of water-loving plants and animals. In the splash zone
of the waterfall look for several primitive plants
representing stages in the history of plant evolution. The
green algae here are aggregations of single cells, while
mosses and liverworts are primitive plants, without
complex internal structures. They all need moist
conditions at some stage of their reproductive cycle. The
polypody fern is more advanced, but has inconspicuous
reproductive structures quite unlike the showy flowers
of the higher plants.

The slow-moving water in the dammed canal (actually
a tributary of the river Glyme) is home to numerous
tadpoles in early summer hence many frogs to be found
in the bank side vegetation later in the year. White
flowered water lilies also grow here, plants which cannot

Frog

tolerate fast moving streams. Another plant growing in the water is mare's tail, with whorls of dark-green strap shaped leaves. It bears flowers, unlike horsetails which may be found on the banks and with which it can be confused. Look for blue-tailed damsel flies resting on the water-side vegetation of pink ragged robin and willow herb, and creamy meadowsweet.

Mare's-tail

Along the bank side in sunny positions, look for clumps of hogweed. These large flat clusters of white flowers are very attractive to many flies, beetles and other insects. Many of the larger flies resemble honey bees with dark brown and orange colouration but are easily recognised by their much faster flight. Others have bright yellow and black stripes and look like wasps. Experiments have shown that this mimicry is effective against being eaten by birds and toads who mis-identify them as "dangerous" stinging insects instead of the harmless flies that they are.

After the path widens and climbs slightly away from the water, look at the plants in the grassland on each side. Under a large beech tree to the right, are several spring flowers which indicate the former presence of ancient woodland; white flowering wood anemone and sanicle and yellow goldilocks buttercup. This last is a relative of the common meadow buttercup but can be distinguished by its distorted flowers, often with less than the normal five petals.

Notice how the shade cast by the trees in the woodland to the left tends to inhibit many of the small flowering plants from growing there. Some large plants, like beech trees and nettles, respond to permanent shade by producing large thin leaves compared to the normal smaller, thicker ones, the different types being more effective for photosynthesis under alternative conditions.

Further along the grassland contains plants which are all able to convert nitrogen from the air into organic nitrogenous plant constituents. Clover, black medick, bush vetch and bird's foot trefoil all have roots which may form nodules loaded with nitrogen-fixing bacteria for this purpose.

Goldilocks buttercup

6. SP369278

At the tarred road, turn right over the bridge. Walk uphill on this road, past farm buildings to the public road.

The estate road is bordered by fine specimens of copper beech while around the lake are groups of Scots pines. The bridge was designed by Thomas Archer when the stream was widened and dammed in about 1750 to create two ornamental lakes.

Large patches of bulrushes grow in the water here. This name is often incorrectly used for the great reed mace frequently depicted in paintings of "Moses in the bulrushes".

Over the bridge and uphill, the meadows to the right are colourful in summer with the flowers of three closely related plants, all members of the pink family. Ragged robin, white and bladder campions all have the bases of their petals fused to make a tube. Bladder campion has white flowers but is easily distinguished from its

Heythrop Park bridge

79

Bladder campion

relatives by the inflated bladder, formed by fused sepals at the base of the flower.

Pause to look back at the house and grounds. The extensive lawns and tree planting produces quite a different landscape and atmosphere compared to the agricultural fields along the rest of the route.

7. SP374275

At the road turn right and walk to the junction. Here turn right and follow the road back to Church Enstone. At the end of the road turn right, then right again to return to the church lych gate.

This lane is called Green Lane. There is evidence of prehistoric and Roman presence in this area and part of Green Lane, now disused, may have its origins as a

Roman road. Its line can be traced for many miles on the map, in places often no more than a track or even a field boundary. The lane may well have been a drove road used to drive cattle or sheep to or from Banbury market. Banbury was, and still is, a major livestock market and drovers brought animals there from Wales. Routes like this were used by drovers for many years after the more major roads were improved by turnpiking. This saved them from paying tolls on their animals, as well as safeguarding the animals from faster traffic and allowing them to graze as they travelled.

The hedgerows along the lane contain a good variety of different types of shrubs. Ash, elder, blackthorn, holly, hazel and dogrose all occur here and would suggest quite an old hedge. However care must be taken in trying to date hedges by the number of species present (see introduction).

The wide verges contain many flowers including woolly thistle, sweet rocket, cranesbill, poppies and hardheads. The conservation value of roadside verges, because of their relatively undisturbed conditions, is now recognised by many biological conservation organisations. In Oxfordshire, as in other counties, some verges are designated as nature reserves because of their botanical interest.

Looking over the stone walls, there are good views of the surrounding countryside. The agricultural landscape of fields, with crops or grazing animals on the lower slopes, contrasts with areas of woodland and copses of planted conifers, which are relatively recent additions to the view. In early summer, the splashes of bright yellow rape flowers reflect changes in traditional crop patterns while the often crumbling and decrepit stone walls show the loss of manpower on the land, the walls now more often replaced with post and wire fences.

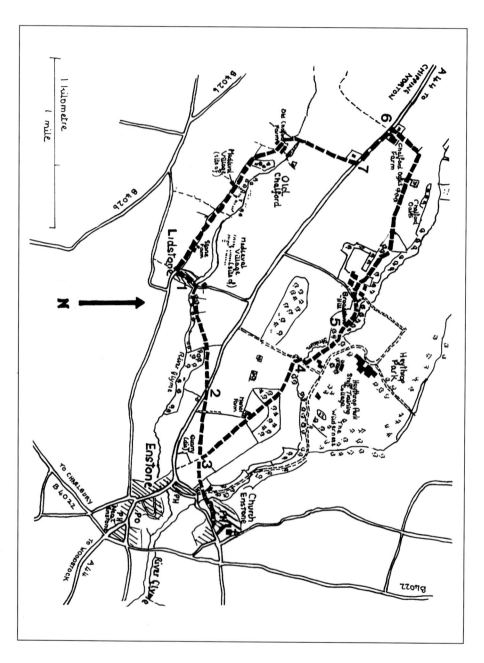

Key – see page 24.

WALK 5

Lidstone

5.5 miles   9 km

(6.5 miles   10.5 km starting at Church Enstone)

This is a varied walk which explores part of two quiet valleys separated by a busy road so there is a small amount of road walking involved. The going is easy although there may be very muddy stretches during wet weather.

1. SP356248

Starting from Lidstone, (limited parking only) take the footpath signed to Church Enstone in the valley bottom close to the bridge. It leads first through a private nature reserve following the line of the stream, so please keep to the path. Continue through a wooded area to emerge onto fields.

ALTERNATIVE START from the lych gate at Church Enstone. Take the road leading downhill past The Crown public house and continue on the tarmac path past the farm buildings. Past the end house take the steep path by the handrail up and across the entrance to Heythrop Park. Bear left and walk up to a stile with a wooden fence on your left. Cross the stile and take the path to the right of a fenced paddock. Cross another stile taking the path ahead across a field. Over another stile in a stone wall, turn right through a gate to join the bridleway leading to Manor Farm at Point 3.

The nature reserve contains a good mix of habitats with boggy ground close to the infant River Glyme, shady woodland and hedgerow. Each habitat supports characteristic plants and animals. In summer on the wet ground, look for great willow herb, with downy leaves and stems, ragged robin and marsh thistle, all with pink flowers; figwort has dark red, almost brown small flowers. Marsh marigold is bright yellow and flowers much earlier than the others. All these plants have roots tolerant of water-logging, whereas most other plants cannot survive such conditions and die either through fungal disease or death of the roots through poor oxygen supply in the wet soil.

Ragged robin

The presence of specialised plants such as these provides a habitat for specific insects. The willow herb is attacked by a small metallic green beetle, belonging to a group called jewel beetles. They are hard to catch as they deliberately fall off the leaf when disturbed. Their larval stages, which are small, shiny and very soft, black grubs, graze on the surface of the leaf, often without making a complete hole, but resulting in large brown patches when the leaf tissue dries out and dies. The dark red flowers of figwort are attractive to wasps which pollinate them, but amongst the flower buds may be found a small greyish beetle with a black spot on its back and a long 'nose'. This last feature is characteristic of a very large family of beetles called weevils. It feeds on the leaves, often making a large number of holes. It uses its 'nose', the rostrum, for biting a hole in the plant and then pushing its eggs into this for protection.

The wooded area also provides conditions which encourage specific insects. The dappled shade is favoured by scorpion flies which use the sunny spots as territories and basking places. These flies get their name from the swollen and upward curving tail of the male, which resembles a scorpion's sting. However these insects are quite harmless and do not sting. When courting, the male will catch and kill a small insect which he takes to the female to eat so that she can judge how good a breeding partner he is.

In the woodland, notice that many of the trees grow from several stems indicating that, in the fairly recent past, the area was cut and cleared. The trees have grown up from the stumps and are formed from several of the resultant shoots. A large field bank on the left marks the boundary of the agricultural land. Notice how pleasant the woodland is in its own right, with dappled sunshine on bright days, cool still air in summer, varied colours on the branches and the ground in autumn. It is a welcome shelter for many different birds and in spring and early summer listen to the song of chaffinches, chiff-chaffs, robins, blackbirds, blue-tits and great-tits, none of which will be heard in the open fields beyond.

Out of the wood, follow the path ahead across the field to a gap in the hedge. Through this continue with another patch of woodland on the right. At a corner, follow the path diagonally left across the field to a stone stile in the wall which leads on to the road (A44). Cross with care.

2. SP367249

Continue in the same direction as before, following the path diagonally right towards a small gap in the hedge. Soon it crosses a track and leads over a stile. Carry on as before to a stile over a wire fence. Cross this and walk to the stone wall and then left to a metal gate.

If using the ALTERNATIVE START return to Church Enstone here by crossing the stone stile in the wall and retrace your steps to your starting point.

The path you have followed from Lidstone is likely to be a "church path" which historically linked an outlying settlement with the church and larger village close by. The views ahead of Church Enstone bear this out. Sometimes these paths were called "corpse paths", used to take bodies for burial. In some more isolated parts of the country these paths are many miles long, and the remains of stone stands for the coffins to give the pall bearers a rest can still be found.

This path gives a good view of the general area, with rounded hills and river valleys, the typical rolling landscape of the Cotswolds. In the past the Cotswolds were famous for wool production but now you are more likely to see arable or dairy farming. The value of this landscape has been recognised as this region is now officially within the Cotswolds Area of Outstanding Natural Beauty (AONB). This means that when planning decisions are made, the landscape character should be conserved. More locally, look at the pattern of walled and hedged fields which will contrast with the "landscaped" grounds of Heythrop to be seen soon.

Even closer to hand, notice the ground in the fields. The soil is well drained, thanks to the underlying Oolitic limestone. This stone lies close to the surface, hence its use for field walls. It is also easily accessible for quarrying and so has been and still is widely used locally for building. A disused quarry on the right is much smaller than the modern operations which use large-scale machinery for extracting the stone.

3. SP373249

Go through the gate and proceed along the bridleway to Manor Farm. Keep right of the main old buildings, go between the modern barns and continue in the same direction along the bridleway which leads on through woodland. Through the gate at the end, bear diagonally left downhill to a small gate.

This bridleway from Enstone to Heythrop Park is an old route, it appears on the 1797 Davis' map of Oxfordshire but probably originally led to Heythrop village which was moved when the park was laid out in the 18th century.

The woodland appears to be a relatively recent planting and it is not shown on any old maps. Many of the trees are beech, planted in diagonal lines but further along the track there are other species – see how many you can spot. Beech trees produce small triangular shaped nuts called mast which are contained in woody cases. The beech nuts are good food for chaffinches and great-tits as well as for small mammals and squirrels. Mast is not produced every year, but often appears in large quantities in a "mast year". The production may be dependant on the weather, but the vast numbers of seeds produces a glut of food, so ensuring that there are some over which can germinate and so produce more trees. Look out for the birch trees which have been killed by birch polypore fungus. The fungus attacks the tree's tissue just under the bark, eventually forming the kidney shaped fruiting bodies which were used as razor strops and even blotting paper in the past.

Birch polypore fungus

As you cross the field, look across the valley to Heythrop Park. From here you can see the ornamental trees which were planted to form the grounds designed by Thomas Archer in the early 18th century. Further along you may be able to see some of the architectural features later included in his scheme, but from here the impression is of a natural woodland and open ground. This was the earliest example of such landscaping, predating the famous grounds designed by William Kent at nearby Rousham by about thirty years (see walk 4). Today the grounds provide a pleasant view with changing tree colours in spring and autumn. The dark green conifers contrast with the lighter greens, yellows and reds of deciduous trees at different times of the year.

4. SP363258

Through the small gate, turn diagonally right alongside the wire fence through rough grass and bushes to emerge opposite a pond, close to a gate on your right. Through the gate and over the bridge, follow the bridleway to the left, marked by blue arrows, as it winds through the woodland. Follow the main path where it bends sharp left crossing the stream towards the woodland edge.

The scrub covering the steep sided valley bottom marks the course of a feeder stream of the Glyme. Its topography makes it unsuitable for agriculture and today it acts as an excellent wildlife refuge and corridor.

The pond is a recent construction and adds to the wildlife conservation value of this area. Yellow flag, water mint, blue-flowered brooklime and brown-flowered articulated rush grow in the water, adding to the rich flora surrounding the pond which includes ladies smock, knapweed, sheep's sorrel and yellow vetchling. In the grassland look for the bluish-green leaves of a sedge. Its stems are triangular in cross-section compared to the round stems of rushes. An easy way to remember this is to say "Rushes are round, sedges have edges". Later on in the woodland, look out for large clumps of pendulous sedge, with long drooping flower heads.

Pond skaters can be seen running over the surface of the water. They have fringes of hairs on the tips of their legs to spread their weight over the water to stop them sinking. On sunny days you can see this if you look at the insect's shadow on the bottom of the pond. These predatory insects will leap on anything small falling into the water and then suck them dry. On permanent ponds, many adults do not grow wings, but where the pond is liable to dry up the adults are winged so that they can fly to another pond.

As the track leads towards the trees, look for the bright blue flowers of green alkanet which look similar to forget-me-not. It was probably introduced from south-west Europe during the Middle Ages to use the red dye which can be obtained from its roots. The name alkanet is derived from Spanish and Arabic words which mean "little henna plant". The plant is evergreen, which probably explains the other part of its name.

Through the woodland, the ground is covered in early spring by the bright yellow flowers and shiny heart-shaped leaves of lesser celandine. It dies down very quickly so that by the end of May, all evidence of it has

Lesser celandines

gone. It spreads from small bulbils at the base of the leaves.

Besides looking at the plants in this wood, notice the features designed to enhance the grounds during the 18th century. The first to be seen is a square bath house built for the Italian wife of the 1st Earl of Shrewsbury. The Italian fashion at that time was for a cold bath and an artificial stream or rill leading to the bath house. Another feature to be seen is the back of a stone alcove which contained three niches for statues. Both these buildings were in what was known as the "Classical Grove".

18th century stone bath house

5. SP360262

Out of the wood follow the path through two small gates, at the second bearing diagonally left to a gate in the upper fence which leads onto a tarred road. Here walk away from the house and take the first turn to the right along a concrete road alongside some large barns. Continue along this straight track for about a mile, 1.5km when it turns left to finally reach the road beside Chalford Oaks Farm.

Spindle tree

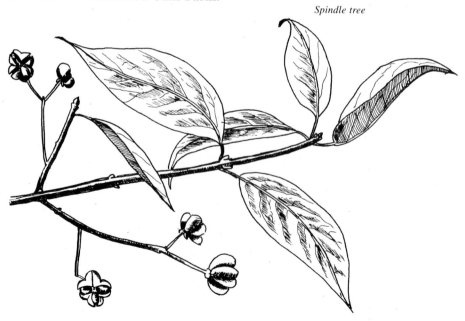

Spindle bushes have been planted in this area. They have insignificant yellow-green flowers but in autumn the very attractive berries have bright pink shells which split to display orange seeds, much liked by robins.

Just after you leave the wood you may see Highland cattle, grazing in the fields. They are distinctive with their shaggy brown coats and large horns. They are a very hardy breed and can do well on poor grazing, in contrast to lowland breeds like Friesians which require good conditions to do well.

There has been a farm here for at least two hundred years, but today it seems that most of the buildings have been rebuilt for non-agricultural purposes, a sign of the changing times in agriculture.

Beyond the buildings, the track goes through farmland, with good views to the right of the Heythrop estate. From this point the open terrain of the parkland

Highland cattle

can be seen, a contrast to the wooded "Wilderness" around the house, glimpses of which can be seen behind you. A recently constructed pond can be seen in the valley, a useful site for wildlife and large enough to attract water fowl.

For some distance along the track you will be able to see Heythrop village across the valley. It is thought that the site of the original village was moved when the park was laid out. The present village was built in the 1870's by Albert Brassey, the then owner of the estate, as a "model" village with well designed good quality houses. The church is also Victorian and replaced a Norman building.

Look out across the valley for an obvious patch of rough ground which, in May, is blue and yellow with bluebells and gorse. In autumn it is tawny with the rich brown of dying bracken. This area is now called Ovens Gorse, but in the last century was Dunthrop Common, Dunthrop being a hamlet beyond Heythrop village. It is unlikely that bluebells would have flourished there when it was commonland, as they cannot tolerate grazing or trampling by animals. Gorse, on the other hand, is a typical plant of commons. It can withstand grazing because of its prickles and, in some places, was actively encouraged by planting to be used as fuel. The name gorse is derived from the Anglo-Saxon *gorst* meaning "a waste", the other word for commons. Furze, the alternative name for the plant, is derived from another Anglo-Saxon word *fyrs* meaning firewood.

Alongside the path is a recently planted copse which contains many native trees and shrubs, including spindle, field maple, oak, hazel, sloe and hawthorn. In the past there was a large wood here called Chalford Oaks Wood, now reduced to two small remnants, so this planting goes some way to replace this lost woodland.

When the path turns left, it passes between thick hedges, which are cut into an A-shape, with a wide base and tapering top. This is a good conservation feature as it encourages the hedge to produce a dense base, and provide more shelter for wildlife. There is a mixture of species in this hedge, which implies that it is several hundred years old.

6. SP341268

When you reach the road, cross with care, turn left and walk along the verge for about 0.25 mile, 0.5 km.

There are many flowers along this verge in summer including meadow geranium with blue flowers, and purple knapweed. The hedge on the right contains many species whereas, even without looking closely it can be seen that the one on the left is quite new and contains only hawthorn.

7. SP345264

Just past the bungalow, turn right down the bridleway to Old Chalford. Through the gate at the bottom, continue between two ponds (see below) and then bear left uphill to the farm. Go through the gate and left past the buildings, following the arrows. Eventually the path reaches a stile. Over this bear right to the right-hand corner of the field to another stile. Follow the path along the top of the fields until it reaches the road at Lidstone. Here turn left downhill, through the village until you reach your starting point.

The bridleway leads back down to the Glyme valley and to an area which is of great historical interest. The present buildings of Old Chalford Farm are now the only habitation here but during the Middle Ages there were two villages situated on opposite sides of the valley, a little further along the route. Past the farm look out for bumps in the fields and also for patches of nettles. They can be seen most clearly when the sun is low in the winter or when the grass is short. On this side of the river the settlement was Nether Chalford and across the river was Over Chalford or Broadstone. It seems that in 1279 there were about 20 households in the two villages and they were still in existence in 1471 when they were

Lidstone cottages

acquired by Oriel College, Oxford. The College let them
out and records indicate that the previously large open
fields had at least been partly enclosed and the
population greatly reduced. By 1536 the Chalfords were
entirely pasture, probably with no arable or buildings
surviving. It is not known whether the present farm was
re-established later or if one house survived throughout
(see Introduction).

These changes were gradual and took many years to
occur. Today events move faster and there have been
recent alterations to this part of the valley. The pond on
the right seen beside the bridleway and the larger lake
further down the river were constructed during the late
1980's by partially damming the river, as at Kiddington,
Glympton and Blenheim. The pond to the left of the
bridleway is older and is a relict of the water mill which
was situated nearby.

During and since World War II, many thousands of

farm and other ponds have either been filled in, drained or overgrown so these ornamental lakes provide a habitat for water birds and other animals. You may see coots, moorhens, mallard and Canada geese here. Canada geese were introduced to this country in the 17th century as an ornamental bird in the collection of Charles II in St James's Park, London. Since then, escaped birds have established themselves countrywide and the population is estimated at 40-50,000 birds. These large numbers are now causing problems because of grazing in agricultural areas and mess in public parks.

As you walk through Lidstone, look out for buildings which are now being used for a different purpose to that for which they were built. The Methodist Chapel is now a garage and close to the start of the walk the house opposite was originally a water mill for grinding corn.

If you started from Church Enstone, continue along the route following the directions from Point 1.

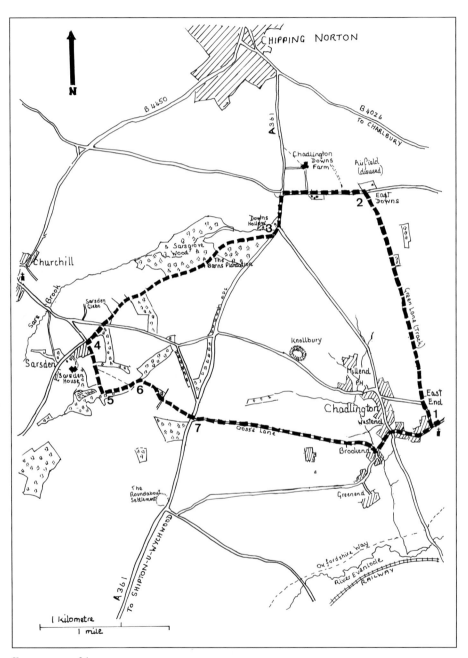

Key – see page 24.

Chadlington

8 miles 13 km

This is an easy walk with no difficult route-finding. By way of green lanes and quiet roads, it leads mostly through rolling agricultural countryside with wide-ranging views, alternating with areas of woodland around Sarsden. There is one short stretch on the A361 which can be busy, but the verges are wide so it is not too difficult.

1. SP333220

Starting in the main street of Chadlington at East End near the church, take Church Road which leads gently uphill past the village school and cottages. At a sharp left hand bend in the road, carry straight on, up the unmetalled road for about 1.5 miles, 2.5km.

Chadlington is an old settlement; its name originally meant "Ceadla's farm". It is mentioned in the Domesday Book of 1086, when there were two landowners, both of whom were officers of the king. One was Reginald, the archer, and the other was Siward Hunter, who had held the land prior to the Norman invasion. Their occupations may have been linked to the proximity of the Royal Wychwood Forest but this is supposition only! Now Chadlington is a sprawling village, made up of several hamlets or "ends" – Eastend, Westend,

Pied wagtail

Brookend, Greenend and Millend, some of which you
will see along the walk.

Close to the turn for Church Road, notice the stone
building opposite which is roofed with Stonesfield slate.
It is covered with mosses and yellow stonecrop. When
this colourful vegetation decays, it provides nourishment
for insect grubs, which in turn are food for birds such
as wagtails and spotted flycatchers. The latter are likely
to nest in the creepers and trellises on the garden walls.
Only the young birds are spotted; the sparrow-sized
adults are more easily recognised by their feeding antics
as they dart from a perch to seize a fly and immediately
return to the same spot.

The unmetalled track is called Green Lane and is one
of several tracks which led from the village to the downs
on the hills around prior to inclosure in 1825. The farm
names of East Downs and Chadlington Downs evoke
that past landscape. Much of the land was used for sheep
pasture, although the zig-zag pattern of the fields
bordering the parish to the east (look on your Ordnance
Survey map if you have one) indicates that this land was
already in cultivation when the parish boundary was
agreed, well before the coming of the Normans in 1066.
The pattern reflects the shape of the early medieval strip

Spotted flycatcher

fields. After inclosure, there were alterations to the road lay-out in other parts of the parish, but this one remains as a by-way.

The views along this track show something of the history of this landscape. The oldest feature to be seen is Knollbury to the left opposite a plantation just below the horizon. The rectangular earthworks of Knollbury date probably from the Iron Age. The suffix "bury" is derived from the Old English word *burh* meaning fort. They are protected by English Heritage because of their archaeological value and by English Nature and the Countryside Commission for their botanical interest. The farmland surrounding the earthworks has been entered into the Countryside Stewardship scheme whereby the farmer receives payment for managing the land to benefit wildlife. An obvious change is the summer display of wild flowers. Look out for more views of this towards the end of the walk as you return to Chadlington. To the right are the woodlands of Ditchley and Dean, some of which are relics of the Royal Forest of Wychwood whose largest remnant clothes the skyline behind you across the valley. The fields evoke the landscape of open grazing land and large fields farmed in common which dated from the early Middle Ages until the early 19th century (see Introduction). The scattered isolated farms are likely to date from the inclosures. New farms were laid out on land previously farmed or grazed in common which was then allotted to various landowners.

The verges along the track contain many plants which would have grown on the downland or on the field edges

Wild onion

Broomrape

prior to modern intensive farming. Two unusual plants to look for in mid-summer are wild onion and broomrape. Wild onion or crow garlic has dark purple flower-heads which are mixed with little bulbils. If eaten by cattle it produces a garlic taste to the milk. Broomrape, as its name suggests, is parasitic. It does not photosynthesise so its green leaves are replaced by brownish scales, a similar colour to the flowers. It parasitises the roots of members of the pea family, (*Leguminosae*) such as trefoils and vetches, and the daisy (*Compositae*) family, including knapweed and thistles. See how many potential plant hosts you can find along these verges.

These grassy verges support several members of the "Brown" (*Satyridae*) family of butterflies, including the meadow brown, ringlet and marbled white. The adult butterflies have conspicuous eye-spots at the edge of their wings, a device to divert attacking birds away from the more vulnerable body parts. Butterflies are regularly used as indicators to monitor changes in insect communities because they are easy to see and record. Bare field edges and use of insecticides have led to considerable reduction in butterfly numbers in recent decades. Modern recommendations to leave unsprayed field edges or headlands have served to increase butterfly and other insect populations along with flowers, birds and other animals.

As well as the well-known blackberry or bramble you may spot the dewberry, a close relation. These berries have a waxy bloom and fewer, but larger segments. The leaves are always divided into three leaflets unlike the blackberry which usually has five.

2. SP326249

When the track reaches the road turn left and walk to the junction where you turn left on to the A316. Continue past the next junction where you take the right fork. Look for the bridleway to the right situated off a small lay-by.

On the right along the minor road was a wartime

Black knapweed   *Greater knapweed*

airfield, one of many small airfields in this area. This one was used in 1940 for training fighter pilots for the Battle of Britain and between 1942 and 1945 for Commonwealth pilots for Bomber Command on night-flying missions. There are remains to be seen in the form of corrugated iron hangers, now used as farm buildings, a brick control tower and parts of runways, now slowly reverting back to nature as they become covered with mosses and stonecrop.

The right-hand verge has two species of knapweed growing side-by-side. Black knapweed, or hard head, has strap shaped leaves while greater knapweed has divided leaves and a ring of large florets around the thistle-like flowerhead.

3. SP315244

Go through a small gate and follow the bridleway through the woodland, The Barns Plantation, keeping the majority of the trees on your left. After a time, you will leave the plantation and reach Sarsgrove Wood on your right. Carry on until the bridleway becomes a road at the end of the wood.

As the name suggests, The Barns Plantation is a

Violets

relatively recent addition to the landscape, whereas Sarsgrove Wood is a much older woodland. The Plantation lacks the rich woodland flora which can be glimpsed in Sarsgrove Wood; primroses, wood anemone, violets, yellow archangel, ramsons and wood spurge make a colourful spring display indicating the antiquity of this wooded site. Larch has been planted here as a plantation tree, producing long straight trunks for timber. It is the only native deciduous conifer; its needles turn bright yellow in autumn and the new spring growth is a soft bright green. These colour variations mean that larch is often used to soften the dark green of evergreen conifer plantations. In winter when the ground flora has died back, notice the large bank and ditch along the wood edge. This marked the boundary in the past when the bank would have been much higher and topped with a wooden palisade to act as a barrier against deer.

Out of the woodland, on a clear day there is a panoramic view ahead and to the right. Stow-on-the-Wold is situated on the ridge on the far skyline while closer by is the distinctive tower of All Saints in Churchill. This was re-built in 1826, modelled on the gabled tower of Magdalen College Oxford, by James

Sarsden stone cross

Langston, who lived in nearby Sarsden House. Churchill was the birth place of William Smith, the renowned 19th century geologist and surveyor who first drew attention to the significance of the layering of rock formations deposited over millions of years. The earliest geological maps of Britain were based on his surveys.

Continue to a junction where you cross the road and carry on in the same direction. At the next junction, where there is a medieval stone cross, take the bridleway to the left, between a Victorian letterbox and a stone pillar.

4. SP291233

Follow the bridleway, now part of the D'Arcy Dalton Way, past Sarsden Home Farm.

Sarsden House itself, in the distance to the right, was rebuilt by William Walter in 1689 after a fire. The park with its serpentine lake and wilderness was landscaped by Humphrey Repton in 1795, another example of a picturesque landscape (see Introduction). The house was remodelled again in 1825 by G.S. Repton, for James

Langston who was a very forward looking land owner. Farms on his estate were run as "model" farms, meaning that they used the most modern technology of the time. Langston was one of the first in the county to use a reaping machine. The tall tower attached to the barn may have housed a boiler for a steam-driven engine used to thresh corn before the era of combine harvesters.

The large copper beech in the paddock to the left is a variety of the more usual native beech. This coloured variety was first found in a German wood about 150 years ago and since then has been used as an ornamental tree in parks and gardens.

Go through a gate and continue down hill with a fence on the right. At the bottom you will enter a small woodland and the path passes over a small causeway over the dam which forms the lake in the grounds beyond the fence to the right.

There are two species of evergreen trees in this area which, like the copper beech, are now widely used as ornamental trees. Lawson's cypress is named after the Edinburgh nurseryman who first imported the tree into Europe from North America in 1854. There are now many varieties in form and coloured foliage to be found in parks and gardens. The other tree, the yew, is native to Britain and seems to have had some religious significance long ago. Following its famed use for the long bows of the army of Henry V at Agincourt, it gradually developed a use as an ornamental tree, particularly for clipped hedges and for topiary because of its dense foliage and relatively slow growth. Both these evergreen trees have protective mechanisms to reduce predation of the seeds by animals. The seeds of the yew are highly poisonous, while those of the cypress are protected within tough scales of cones, only being exposed when they are mature and ready to be dispersed.

5. SP293227

Opposite a padlocked gate, look for a path to the left, which leads through the woodland. After about a third of a mile or about half a kilometre, look for a

path to the right (just past a gate in the metal fence on the left).

Along this path during the summer months, you are likely to disturb small frogs and toads. These closely related amphibians differ in that the toad has a drier, warty skin and is able to survive in quite dry places such as under fallen logs, in crevices in walls or in holes in the ground. The frog has much moister skin and needs to hide in damp vegetation. Frogs are the prey for many animals including badgers, stoats, weasels, hedgehogs, herons, crows and grass snakes. The toad is far better protected by mucus which is secreted when it is attacked and which most animals find distasteful.

During late summer and autumn some of the trunks of both living and dead deciduous trees may bear the large, pale-brown, scaly fruiting bodies of the dryad's saddle fungus. Its cap resembles a flat seat or saddle with creamy white pores on the underside which shed spores dispersing the fungus to nearby new host trees.

6. SP297228

When you turn right the path leads through woodland for a short distance, then emerges onto a field. Take the path diagonally left to the edge of the plantation, then turning right, follow the field edge to a tarred track. Go straight on across the next field to the road. At the road cross with care and take the lane opposite.

In the first field, pause to look back across the parkland around Sarsden, which will be especially clear to see in the winter. The tall, spreading trees in the grassland contrast with the open spaces of the agricultural fields, bordered by neat hedges. The copse at the edge of this field is a typical example of a disused small local quarry, now overgrown and planted with trees.

7. SP304223

The lane leads downhill. It is not busy but be aware of traffic all the same.

The line of pollarded ash trees makes a fine feature in this otherwise rather bare landscape. Ash timber is hard and elastic and traditionally was put to use as handles for axes and other tools, oars and garden forks. It is the only timber which burns well as green wood.

To the left look for more views of Knollbury earthwork – see start of walk.

This road, although attractive with its flowery verges and stone walls, is not an old route like the byway at the start of the walk. It was laid out when Chadlington was enclosed in 1825 and replaced an earlier route which was probably hedged rather than walled. When the road curves slightly to the left towards the bottom of the hill, it rejoins the old route. Notice that this old section of the lane is different to the rest. It winds between high banks with old mixed hedges, containing some woodland plants, a marked contrast to the thin hedges or stone walls bordering the road further back.

The road leads to Brookend, where you can pause for a moment beside the flower-bordered stream. Take the left turn uphill and, at the next junction, take the middle road (not sharp right) to return to the starting point.

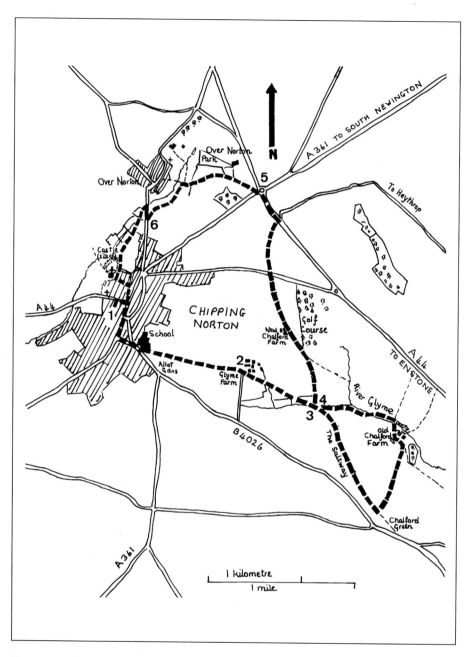

Key – see page 24.

WALK 7

Chipping Norton

7.5 miles 12 km

Short cut 5 miles 8 km

This walk leads through varied countryside with several areas of landscape and botanical interest. It follows an ancient track for some distance and the going is easy, but may be muddy after wet weather. The route is a figure of eight so can easily be shortened.

1. SP313271

Start from the public car park behind New Street in Chipping Norton. Turn right out of the car park, then right again. Continue to the King's Arms and turn left here bearing right along the Burford Road. After about 400 yards/metres, look out for the footpath sign just past Chipping Norton School beside the car park. The path leads close to the school buildings, then along a track with allotments on the right, until you reach Glyme Farm.

Both the start and finish of this walk are close to the market place which gave Chipping Norton its name, Chipping or Chepping being the old word for market. However the settlement is much older than the market as there is evidence of a Romano-British settlement close by between the 2nd and 4th centuries AD. This was a good place for habitation as it is situated on the springline between the Oolitic limestone and the impervious lias clay, hence there was always a reliable water supply.

Chipping Norton Town Hall and Market Place

At the start of the track in the allotments on the right, grows Canadian golden-rod, which has probably escaped from a garden. Studies have shown that golden-rod can live for several hundred years. The clumps grow larger but die off in the centre, eventually forming a large ring of small clumps, rather in the way that a fairy-ring fungus grows. Foreign plants which escape from gardens can often become serious weeds in the countryside. This is because they are not growing in their normal conditions where animals or insects eat them or disease prevents them from spreading too much. Rhododendron is a classic example of this and is now a serious problem in parts of Wales and Devon.

As well as foreign wild flowers becoming prized in gardens, some of our native species are too. The blue flowered meadow cranesbill or geranium is one such plant and you will see many of these along this path. There are several types of geraniums along this route including hedgerow cranesbill and herb Robert. They all have five petals and if you crush a leaf they all have a strong smell caused by chemicals which deter animals from eating them. Meadow cranesbill is a plant which prefers a lime-rich soil as do many others which can be seen here like knapweeds, ladies bedstraw, scabious and the occasional sainfoin. This last is a striking plant with tall spikes of pink flowers and was grown as a "hay" plant in the past. "Sain" is the French word for hay. It is a legume or member of the pea family and so was also used as a soil improver, adding nitrogen to the soil.

The plentiful supply of limestone can be seen here as the track and many of the fields nearby have stone walls. The field boundaries in this immediate area are a mixture of walls and hedges. Almost everywhere else in Oxfordshire hedges are usual but, further west into the Cotswolds, walls predominate.

2. SP327264

At the farm there is a junction of tracks. Take the stile on the right and continue slightly diagonally right across two more stiles until you reach a stile and footbridge over a stream.

The buildings of Glyme Farm reflect the changing use of building materials over the years. There is the stone of the original farm with slate for roofing contrasting with metal sheeting.

These fields are well managed both for walkers and wildlife. The paths are kept open by mowing so that crops are not damaged by walkers. The banks of the steep field beyond the stream are medieval strip lynchets, formed by ploughing so as to provide level terraces for crops. It is a similar formation to ridge-and-furrow in level fields. The use of steep marginal land probably occurred during the late 13th century when the population reached a high point before being reduced by the Black Death in the mid 14th century.

Past the stream, carry on in the same direction diagonally right across a steep slope to a stile crossing into an area of recent tree planting. The path continues in the same direction over two further stiles across fields with more tree planting. The third field contains a ruined building which you should keep on the right hand side. The path leads to the far corner of the field where a stile by a gate leads into a green lane.

The areas of tree planting will allow wildlife to flourish. The grass between the small saplings encourages many butterflies such as the small heath which is common here, its caterpillars feeding on the narrow leaved grasses. The grass also provides cover for voles, mice and shrews, although a sharp-eyed barn owl or kestrel may pick them off. In time the trees will grow to form a small copse and other plants and animals will start to colonise the area.

Some of the fields have been planted with particular types of grass. Crested dog's tail is a small grass with the flowers and seeds all facing one way on the stem. Cocksfoot is a much larger grass forming tussocks. Its greenish-purple flower heads are arranged on three stems, a central one and two side shoots, giving the appearance of a bird's foot, hence the name.

In both the steep grazed field just past the stream and the meadow beside the ruin you may spot a plant which is quite rare in Britain. It has spikes of blue flowers similar to those of sage and is called meadow clary, another plant which prefers a lime-rich soil. Notice how the garden plants and shrubs, such as lilac, around the ruin have survived longer than the building, the remains of an earlier New Chalford Farm which disappeared during the last century. There is a "new" New Chalford Farm further along the walk! Chalford means "chalk stream ford"; it is a common placename in similar settings.

3. SP334260

Over the stile, turn right and walk along the lane for just over 1km or about three-quarters of a mile until you reach a bridleway leading left through a metal gate.

SHORT CUT
For a shorter walk turn left when you reach the green lane. Ignore section 3 (except for information about this track, the Saltway) and rejoin at Point 4.

This green lane is called the Saltway. It is an ancient track which was originally used for transporting salt from Droitwich in the West Midlands, possibly linking, via Akeman Street, with Princes Risborough at the foot of the Chilterns in Buckinghamshire. Later, it was a drove road used by herds of cattle and flocks of sheep travelling across country making use of existing tracks and avoiding the tolls on the turnpike, the route of the present A44. It is now officially classed as a byway ie a road now used as a footpath.

Opposite the stile leading on to the Saltway is a nature reserve managed by the Berkshire, Buckinghamshire and Oxfordshire Naturalists' Trust (see comments at the end of Section 3).

The track is quite shady in places and this results in moist ground and lower temperatures. Creeping buttercup is abundant here as is red-flowered woundwort whose leaves contain antiseptic compounds used by herbalists to treat bites and scratches, hence its name. Look out for germander speedwell, wood avens, herb Robert and black bryony with glossy heart shaped leaves and clusters of poisonous red berries in autumn. The hedges bordering the track contain tree and shrub species such as hazel, field maple, wayfaring tree, sloe, elder and hawthorn; this rich mixture gives rise to vivid autumn colours, particularly the golden yellow of field maple. This tree is related to the American maples which are famed for their brilliant colours in the "fall". The hedges provide shelter for birds and insects, many of

Blackcap

which do not like the exposed windy conditions in the fields. You may hear wrens, robins, chaffinches, tits and blackcaps and may see birds flying along the track ahead of you rather than into the fields. Yellow brimstone butterflies can be seen in early spring and the autumn; they hibernate as adults through the winter and so are the earliest butterflies to be seen. Speckled wood butterflies like sunny spots in dappled sunlight for basking; their caterpillars feed on grasses in shady places.

Follow the bridleway downhill to Old Chalford Farm. At the farm turn left through the farm buildings, following the blue arrows. Continue downhill following the track which leads between the two lakes to a gate on your left just past the lakes.

When you turn left off the track and head down to the farm there are wide views to be seen. Heythrop House, surrounded by woodland is ahead to the right, and the A44 is on the skyline, the old turnpike which the drove road avoided. To the far right is the large grain silo, visible from many of the walks in this book and to the left is Chipping Norton golf course, both modern additions to the countryside. One reflects the high production of grain, thanks to modern agricultural methods, and the other, the results of this success with land being used for purposes other than traditional agriculture.

In this area you may see an old breed of cattle, the Longhorn. They have a distinctive white stripe along their backs and large spreading horns. They were useful, all-purpose cattle, good as draught animals as well as producing milk and meat. This farm has many unusual beef cattle which may be seen on Walk 5 as well.

In warm weather, the still water in the lakes may be covered with blanket weed, alga whose growth is stimulated by nitrates and other fertilizers seeping into the water. This demonstrates the need for a NSA (Nitrate Sensitive Area). Several farms in this area have entered a pilot scheme aimed at reducing the level of nitrate in the water system. This has involved either abandoning the use of nitrate fertilizer completely and switching from arable to grassland, or partly reducing artificial fertilizer applications and careful control of the use of farmyard manure. This will reduce the amount of nitrate leaching into the River Glyme headwaters which supplement the domestic water supply in this area. Participating farmers receive compensation to offset reductions in crop yields.

Take the turning through the gate on the left and walk along the field parallel to the lake and stream. After passing through two gateways, look out for the arrows which indicate the path turning left over the stream. Continue in the same direction as before, up the valley alongside the stream to reach a gate which leads back onto the Saltway. Here turn right.

Walking along the field edge beside the river, you will see different plants to those in dry fields. Ragged robin and yellow flag grow along the fence line as well as abundant creeping buttercup, all plants which like moist ground. Another one, seen in spring, is marsh marigold with bold yellow flowers. A number of different thistles can be seen, including the small creeping thistle and the tall slender marsh thistle with dark leaves and purple or occasionally white flowers. Musk thistles have large,

Musk thistle

nodding flower heads and their slightly musky fragrance is attractive to bees, hoverflies and butterflies.

Further along when the stream is on your right, the area of limestone grassland and scrub on the valley-side beyond the stream is a nature reserve managed by BBONT, the Berkshire, Buckinghamshire and Oxford-shire Naturalists' Trust. It is part of a larger SSSI (Site of Special Scientific Interest) around the headwaters of the River Glyme. The rare limestone grassland is one of only a few patches that now remain on the edge of the Cotswolds and contrasts with the short grazed fields nearby. It is gradually being invaded by hawthorn bushes and other young trees. If left unmanaged, it will become overgrown with scrub and evolve into woodland.

4. SP334260

(SHORT CUT Walk left here as described at the start of Point 3).

Emerging once more on the Saltway, turn right and walk along the track as it climbs uphill. Through the small wooden gate into a field, follow the path diagonally to the left towards the house in the distance. Continue along the farm track and cross the road with care. Continue along the track opposite until another road is reached. This is the main A44. Turn left here and walk along the pathway to the roundabout.

Here the path is quite narrow, but you can see that the hedges are set back and that the track has become overgrown due to reduced traffic along it.

The golf course on the right is probably situated on ground which is not good for agriculture. Early in the 19th century this area was called Wheelers Heath and was commonland with rough vegetation used for grazing and fuel collection. Some parts of the golf course probably have a similar vegetation to those days and are potentially good areas for wildlife, but the greens are heavily treated with chemicals to ensure a smooth surface so, like most golf courses, is a mixed blessing in the countryside. The farm on the left is called New

Chalford Farm and obviously replaces the ruined one seen earlier further down the valley.

The farm track has been planted with a line of young lime trees which in time will grow to form a shady avenue, like that to be seen along the road ahead. Some types of lime grow a "skirt" of bushy shoots around their base, a good aid to identification. A particular species of aphid, the lime aphid, lives on lime trees and a large tree may have several million insects on it in a good summer. They produce huge quantities of sugary waste fluids which drop onto the leaves, giving them a shiny surface. If this is not washed off by the rain, it grows a black fungus, thus making the tree look very grimy. The aphids are food for the larvae of many other insects including ladybirds and hoverflies.

Across the road the track continues, rather wider then before, thus allowing the light to encourage more flowering plants.Cow parsley, hogweed, rosebay willowherb, dog rose, St John's wort and crosswort can all be seen during the warmer months. Cross wort has pale yellow flowers and whorls of four leaves along its stem, which give rise to its name. It is related to the well known cleavers or goose-grass.

Flowering at different times of the year reduces competition for light and growing space, so permitting a greater variety of plants. In turn this provides a continuous sequence of food for animals and insects, which base their life cycles round their food supply. Hedgerows and verges such as this with their variety of damp and dry, sunny and shaded places are essential for wildlife and contrast markedly with the cultivated fields containing crops which all flower and produce seed at the same time. This is why conservationists value hedgerows and field edges; their variety is important for encouraging diversity in the small and often unseen wildlife as well as the more obvious birds, butterflies and attractive flowers.

The nettles along this track indicate nitrogen-rich soil. This is often associated with human and animal use in the past, and so demonstrates the still present effect of the drove herds of the past (see Walk 8). Young nettle

Rosehips

shoots can be eaten in salads and older shoots used to produce a greenish-yellow dye for cloth. Other plants along the track are also often used in the kitchen. The most obvious is blackberries which can be used for jam and jelly as well as in puddings. Rosehips are used for making syrup. During the Second World War and afterwards, this was a rich supply of Vitamin C when other sources were in short supply and country children could earn pocket money by collecting the hips.

Look out for comma butterflies feeding on the sugary juices from damaged fruit in late summer; they are recognised by their ragged wing-shapes and the white comma-shaped mark on the underside of their wings. Wasps chew on the fruit, so making the juices available to flies and other insects which feed on the sweet flesh.

As you walk you may hear a high pitched squeaking in the undergrowth. This is probably a family of common shrews searching for food or a courting male chasing a female. These animals are easy to recognise by their long noses. They are so small that they lose an enormous amount of heat and therefore have to eat almost continuously to keep alive. They are carnivores and feed on worms and insects as a high protein, high energy diet.

5. SP327283

At the roundabout, beside the petrol station, cross the road on the left, leading to Chipping Norton and

take the path opposite through the kissing-gate. Walk through a clump of beech trees then go right, along the path parallel to the fence. At a junction continue along the field edge with trees on the right. Carry on along a grassy track to the bottom of the field, then continue downhill between hedges. 100 yards/metres down the track, opposite a cottage, take the path to the left. Amongst the waterworks behind the wire fence is the remains of a Bronze age round barrow or burial mound, an indication of the long human habitation in this area.

As you walk along the field edge, notice the variety of small flowers. These are often found at the edge of arable fields and are often called "weeds of cultivation". The seeds can stay dormant for many years, but will germinate when brought to the surface by ploughing or other disturbance.The plants grow quickly and flower when small, producing many seeds, so that at least some have a good chance of surviving in future years. However if the ground is not disturbed these plants are quickly overgrown by larger grasses and plants which thrive in undisturbed conditions. The pollen from these "weeds" has been found in ancient peat deposits; it can help to indicate when cultivation of crops first began in prehistory.

As well as modern breeds, you may see some ginger-haired Tamworth pigs in this area. These are an old breed now but were important when pigs were first introduced to Australia. Their coloured hair and skin protected them from the strong sun there, whereas paler pink pigs often roll in mud to give some protection against sunburn.

Follow the path opposite the cottage through a marshy area, then over a stile. It leads along the bottom of the slope and continues until it reaches the road.

The grassland past the cottage is a very attractive area, and is obviously much used by local people. There are many wild flowers here in the unimproved sward. Amongst the grass tussocks look out for spotted orchids. These plants have fungus associations with their roots and obtain minerals by exchanging nutrients with the fungus so that both flourish, often on impoverished soils. Such associations are vital for assisting young seedlings to survive and establish themselves. Orchids produce huge numbers of very tiny seeds, which store very little food, so the seedlings do not have enough food supplies to survive on their own and need the fungus partnership.

In the damp soil you will find an unusual plant called horsetail with whorls of bright green leaves. They belong to an ancient group of plants abundant about 350 million years ago when the coal measures were being laid down. Their reproductive structures appear in early spring and look like small soft cones produced on the end of a short stalk, a feature which reveals their ancient history.

Further along this part of the path, the fields show obvious remains of ridge-and-furrow cultivation orientated down the slope to assist drainage. Notice how different plants show as coloured stripes, revealing which prefer damp or dry conditions. Along the lower field edge on your right are several massive ash and sycamore trees. The sycamores have rough bark which allows large collections of moss and lichens to grow on them, whereas the ash is much smoother and not so favourable. These isolated trees have grown into their natural shape which aids their identification when the branches are bare in the winter. The ash, with its downwards curving branches, is taller and slimmer than the sycamore. Contrast these trees with the five large limes on the skyline ahead. Their bases have been shaped into a flat line by animals browsing on the foliage, giving them a manicured appearance.

6. SP315279

At the road, turn right and walk along the pavement until you cross a bridge. Here cross the road with care and take the footpath which leads off on the left. Follow the path through a small gate at the end of the field then bear left through trees and a tunnel. Continue along the field edge and through a kissing gate at the end. Go straight on up the track turning slightly right, then left into the churchyard. Opposite

Alms houses

the church turn left up the road past the almshouses on the left. At the junction go right along the edge of the Market Place then right down New Street and back to the carpark entrance.

As you approach Chipping Norton you will see the mound of the Castle on your right. In the 12th century Chipping Norton belonged to the Fitzalan family who were also Lords of Clun in Shropshire. The castle was built during this time but was in ruins by the end of the Middle Ages. It seems that the Fitzalans spent most of their money on their Clun manor which was situated in an area of unrest on the Welsh borders.

The row of eight alms houses were built in 1640 by Henry Cornish, one of the first Burgesses of the town when it received its Royal Charter in 1606.

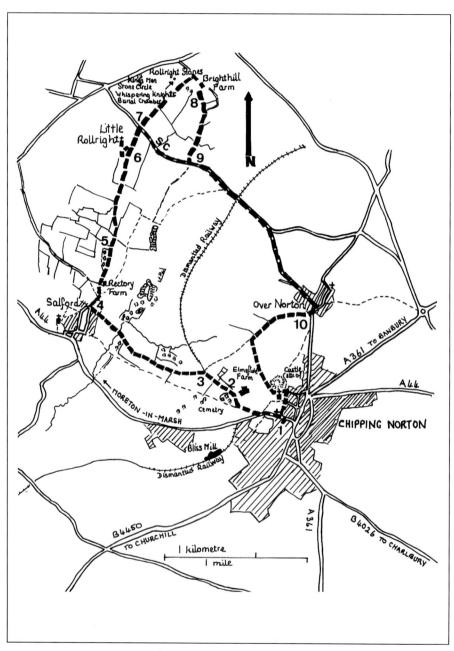

Rollright Stones
King's Men
Stone Circle
Whispering Knights
Burial Chamber
Brighthill Farm
7
8
Little Rollright
SC
6
9
N
5
Dismantled Railway
Rectory Farm
Salford
4
Over Norton
10
A44
A361 TO BANBURY
3
2
Elmsfield Farm
Castle (site of)
MORETON-IN-MARSH
Cemetery
A44
1
CHIPPING NORTON
Bliss Mill
Dismantled Railway
B4450
B4026 TO CHARLBURY
TO CHURCHILL
A361

1 kilometre
1 mile

Key – see page 24.

WALK 8

Salford and Little Rollright

7 miles 11 km

Shorter route 6.5 miles 10.5 km

This walk uses an old byway and quiet country roads, as well as field paths. Within the wide views of pleasant countryside, there are many reminders of the changing impact of human activity on the landscape.

1. SP313271

Start from the public carpark off New Street in Chipping Norton, turning left along the road leading out of the town towards Moreton-in-Marsh (A44). Walking on the right-hand-side of the road, when you reach the playing field, look for the footpath sign on the right through a kissing gate.

Chipping Norton was a centre for the local woollen industry from the 15th century onwards (see also Walk 7). By the 19th century the town was specialising in tweed manufacture, epitomised by the mill of Bliss & Sons, which still stands today. Although it closed in 1980 and is now divided into apartments, the fine Victorian building is still a landmark along this road and can be seen from the playing field .

Follow the path signed to Salford, through another

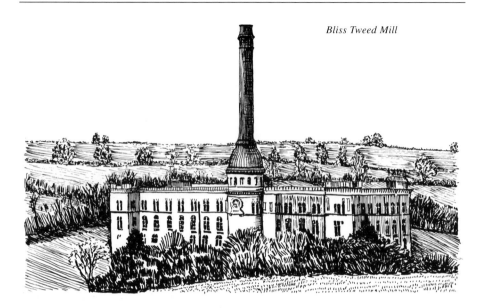

Bliss Tweed Mill

**kissing gate close to the children's play area, then
downhill over a stone footbridge. Take the right-hand
path, bearing slightly right up-hill towards chestnut
trees and a house. You will then cross a track via two
stiles. Follow the path up the field with trees on your
left, to a stile beside a gate.**

The plants growing in the bottom of the valley such
as willow herb and rushes are indicators of wet ground.
Poplars have been planted here; these trees are easily
propagated from cuttings and grow rapidly. They are
often grown as windbreaks and the white timber used
for match making.

The track you cross is bordered with horse-chestnut
trees, which also lined the road from Chipping Norton.
This tree is not native to Britain but was probably
introduced by the Romans. Its timber is soft so has few
uses but the tree provides shade and its distinctive outline
and candle-shaped flowers make it ideal for decorative
purposes. The bluebells seen beneath the trees in spring
are Spanish bluebells with larger, more upright flower
stems and paler blue flowers than the native bluebell
which you will find further on.

2. SP307274

Over the stile, continue straight along the right-hand side of the next two fields; in the second the path becomes a track. When you reach a junction of tracks, turn left on to a grassy track.

At the stile notice the elm saplings growing alongside. If there are leaves on the trees, they are easy to recognise as one side of the leaf extends further down the stalk than the other. In February/March tufts of small red flowers appear on the twigs which later develop into groups of round seeds about the size of a penny. They have flat membranous wings to help them disperse in the wind. There are many types of elm, but English elm produces sterile seeds and relies instead on root suckers to produce new plants.

Pause in the gateway between the two fields and look back at Chipping Norton. Notice the old houses built of local stone in the town centre. They contrast with modern housing on the steeper slopes which does not use local materials. The chimney of Bliss Mill can be seen to the right in winter and on the far skyline the tall lights of the sports ground show how important leisure activities are in the late 20th century.

The hedge on your right alongside this track (and to the left of the one further on) is likely to be very old. It grows on a bank and marks the line of the parish boundary. It is shown on Davis' map of Oxfordshire made in 1797. An indication of its age is in the wide variety of species to be found here including sycamore, elder, sloe, ash and hawthorn. A less common type of hawthorn may be spotted with less dissected leaves and slightly larger flowers. The berries (haws) contain two seeds unlike the one seed found in common hawthorn. This is Midland hawthorn and is often an indicator of old hedges which are remnants of former woodland.

Hawthorn is the commonest hedging shrub, extensively planted during the Parliamentary enclosures in the 18th and 19th centuries. Its spiny, dense growth is a good barrier against animals and especially so when the hedge is managed in the traditional way by laying.

The stems are partially cut, then bent and woven between upright stakes so encouraging thicker growth and filling any gaps. Modern flail cutters don't have the same effect. The blossom played a part in celebrating May Day, the festival marking the coming of spring and planting of crops, hence the alternative name of "May". However the flowers were not to be brought indoors as this was thought to bring bad luck as in the old country saying "May in, coffin out".

3. SP304276

Follow the grassy track as it goes gently downhill, eventually crossing a small stream and walking between two hedges, until you reach Salford.

This track is likely to be part of the old drovers route which provided an alternative to the turnpike through Chipping Norton. It could also be part of the Salt Way leading from Salford (see Introduction). Further on where the track is more enclosed there are many nettles. This indicates that this part of the track may have been used as an overnight stop for drover's flocks or herds; nettles often grow in nitrogen-rich soil made so by animal droppings. However, a recent national survey has shown that nettles are much more common in hedgerow ditches and along stream sides than they used to be because of fertilizers used on farmland, so now sometimes their presence is due to modern rather than ancient influences.

On a clear day there are good views from the track to the right over the valley to the hills behind Little Rollright. From this and other vantage points along the route, notice the subtle differences in the field shapes and patterns. Around Little Rollright, which you will see close at hand later, there are large square fields, laid out in the 15th century when open arable land was converted to sheep pasture. These early inclosures caused considerable economic hardship and hunger to the poorer people of the area which led in 1548 to a serious rebellion led by Henry Joyce, Vicar of Chipping Norton, and three neighbouring priests. The rebellion

Goat willow

was crushed by the local gentry, who were responsible for the inclosures. The Vicar was hanged from the tower of Chipping Norton's church. In Salford parish, inclosure of open fields did not occur until 1770 when the new fields were laid out in rectangular arrangement. As you walk look and see if this difference in inclosure periods is borne out by the differences in hedge species you find (see Introduction).

When the path crosses the small stream, look for the poplars and goat willow growing here, both species liking the wet soil. Goat willow has coarse, broad leaves and produces the familiar fluffy yellow catkins or pussy willow. These are the male flowers and provide a very important food source for many insects, including bumble bees, in early spring. The spiky pale green female catkins are on separate trees and later produce masses of white cotton-covered seeds which float off in the wind. This tree cover provides shelter for many birds which you may hear singing here – blackcap, robin, chaffinch, wren and blackbird, noticeably different to the skylarks of the open fields behind you.

4. SP290282

In Salford, continue straight on until you see a minor road to the right, lined with poplars, signed to Rectory Farm.

The path leads only through the northern tip of Salford, so turn left in the village to see more. The name Salford means "salt ford" indicating that salt was carried through the area. The ford could refer to the stream just crossed or another route slightly to the south. It must have been an important crossing place for the name to have evolved and indicates that the water course was probably much bigger than today.

Walk along the track for about 150 yards/metres until you reach a junction of tracks. Look for the

footpath sign indicating the path which leads diagonally off to the left just past the track to the left. The path crosses a small field to a stile beside farm buildings. Bear slightly left here, then right to walk parallel to the barns with a hedge on your right. Continue along the field edge to a stile leading into woodland. Go left and follow the path through the wood to emerge through a gate at the end.

The woodland is predominantly conifer and includes larch, cypress and spruce. Spruce (Christmas) trees grow by producing a ring of branches around the top of the stem each year. Hence, by counting the number of branch rings, you can age the tree. The distance between branches shows whether the year was good or bad for growth. The trees are planted close together to encourage them to grow straight, but their thick leaves shades out most of the light and very little grows on the woodland floor except moss. This is often torn up by blackbirds and other birds searching for food or nesting material. The undulating ground beneath the trees and in the adjoining grassland shows signs of ridge-and-furrow, so it seems that this copse was planted on part of an old pasture field, which had earlier been derived from an arable open field. There may have been a patch of earlier woodland here before the conifers were planted as there are some large tree stumps to be seen.

5. SP292289

Out of the wood, the path follows the line of a field ditch, soon crossing a wide footbridge on the right, then continuing in the same direction as before with the hedge on your left. The path crosses a stream then leads through another more recent conifer plantation and an area of uncultivated grassland. Go through a small gate, then carry on along a grassy path. Over a stile, the path continues straight on, downhill over the field towards farm buildings.

In the plantation, pheasants are being reared, the trees acting as cover for the birds. You may see a white pheasant, a type which was originally introduced as an

Common spotted orchid

ornamental variety, in the same way as white deer at stately homes. White forms of animals are rare in nature as they are so conspicuous and are therefore soon caught by predators; the normal brownish pheasant colouration is very good camouflage.

In the rough grassy area, there is a wet patch where sedges grow. Amongst the flowers look for common spotted orchids with pink or mauve flowers and leaves with large dark spots. These orchids have an ingenious method of ensuring that their flowers are cross-pollinated to produce vigorous new plants. Visiting bees are attracted by the flower to seek nectar. In so doing, clumps of pollen grains stick to the bee's head with a quick drying natural glue. When other similar orchids are visited, the pollen is deposited on the stigmas to fertilise these flowers.

As you walk notice the variety of fields you can see. In spring and summer, lush grass is grown for silage or hay. For silage the grass is used green, not dried as in haymaking. The green grass is stored so as to ferment, which increases it's nutritive value. This technique was introduced after the last war so this crop is relatively new to the countryside and the old flower-rich hay meadows are now rare in this part of the country. An even more modern phenomenon to be seen are the set-aside fields. This is a complex arrangement whereby farmers are paid a grant to leave a proportion of arable land unproductive to reduce the European Union food surplus. The fields chosen for set aside are changed each year and are often ploughed during the summer to prevent the spread of weeds. The reddish-brown appearance of such fields in summer is due to their having been sprayed with herbicide, again to keep weeds under control.

Notice also the thick sinuous line of shrubs and trees in the valley. This marks the route of the disused railway line, opened in 1887, which once linked Chipping Norton to Banbury and Cheltenham. The line was important for the carriage of iron ore but was closed in 1964 as part of the Beeching closure programme. Now it is a valuable wildlife refuge and corridor.

6. SP295299

When you reach the farm, follow the path through the yard. At the lane turn left, then right, taking the footpath uphill to reach a road.

Along the farm lane, notice the line of walnut trees to the right. Walnut originated in the eastern Mediterranean and has been grown in orchards in England for its nuts since possibly Saxon times. The timber is highly patterned and is greatly valued in furniture making, often being used as a veneer. The plant produces a herbicidal chemical which can wash off its leaves and inhibit some types of plants which may grow around the base of the tree. This can cause problems if the tree is planted in a garden.

This small hamlet is Little Rollright. It is termed a "shrunken" village with only three houses and a church remaining. In the past it was a much larger settlement but became depopulated when farming changed from arable to sheep during the 15th century, so reducing the workforce needed.

Pause to look back at the village from the hillside; you will notice humps and depressions around the hamlet showing where the old buildings were. On the slope beyond the hamlet, notice the patch of uncultivated ground. This marks the springline; several springs feed streams which used to fill fish ponds used during the Middle Ages.

7. SP296303

Cross the main road with care and follow the path straight ahead through the gate. Continue across the next three fields until you reach a track.

SHORT CUT
Turn right at the main road for a shorter route to Over Norton. Rejoin the route at Point 9.

To the left across the second field are the Rollright Stones. These are three different groups of standing stones. The nearest to the path is called the Whispering

The King's Men

Knights and is a burial chamber dating back to the Neolithic period about 4000 years ago. The monument has been protected by a metal fence since 1895.

To see the King's Men stone circle and the single King Stone you can turn left at the track ahead, turning left along the road, returning to the trail by retracing your steps.

The King's Men consists of 77 stones in a circle about 30 metres in diameter. It is thought that some of the smaller stones may have broken off the larger ones and that originally there were only 22 stones. Excavations have shown that the stones are set several feet into the ground. Nobody really knows the function of the circle but it is likely to have been a meeting place, possibly for religious ceremonies. Evidence of human activity has been found in the whole area dating from the late Mesolithic period 6500BC to the Saxons, around 800AD, from the prehistoric burial mounds, Iron Age and Roman agriculture through to a Saxon cemetery.

Like all stone monuments there are numerous legends concerning them. The circle is supposed to represent the army of a Danish king going into battle against the

Saxons and the single stone, the king, who was turned to stone by a witch. The Whispering Knights are a group of dissidents plotting against the king!

At the farm track turn right towards Brighthill Farm. Go past the barns, through the gate and continue to a gate ahead. Go diagonally right downhill to a stile in the far corner of the field.

8. SP303305

The path leads past a new pond then over a stile in the hedge. Turn and follow the field edge to the right. Through the next gap, take the path slightly to the left across the field, emerging onto the road near a small stone bridge where the SHORT CUT rejoins the trail.

The pond in the field corner is a modern one but is a valuable addition to the countryside since so many farm ponds have fallen into disuse and been filled in. The shallow, still, open water provides different conditions for numerous plants and animals compared with flowing ditches, streams and rivers. Many water-loving plants grow at the pond side including meadow sweet with strong smelling leaves and clusters of cream flowers. Water cress also grows at the edge while yellow iris, reedmace and bulrush grow in the water. Reedmace is often mistakenly called bulrush but in fact is quite a different plant. The brown seed heads are pulled apart by birds in the spring looking for nest material. The inside of the stems are used by various moth caterpillars as it is safer living here than on the surface of the leaves where there is a danger of falling into the water. The dark green spiky leaves of the true bulrush show this plant to belong to the family of reeds and sedges. Clusters of brown flowers appear along the 'leaves', showing them to be stems doing the work of leaves. The island in the centre of the pond allows mallard, moorhen and other birds to nest in comparative safety.

Reed mace

Along the field edge past the pond, the stream line is marked by many crack willows. These old trees live up to their name as numerous very heavy branches have